70116869

BEHOLD NOW BEHEMOTH: DINOSAURS ALL OVER THE BIBLE!

Glenn L. Wilson

WestBow
PRESS
A DIVISION OF THOMAS NELSON

WestBow Press books may be ordered through booksellers or by contacting:

WestBow Press
A Division of Thomas Nelson
1663 Liberty Drive
Bloomington, IN 47403
www.westbowpress.com
1-(866) 928-1240

ISBN: 978-1-4497-2639-3 (e)
ISBN: 978-1-4497-2640-9 (sc)
ISBN: 978-1-4497-2641-6 (hbk)

Library of Congress Control Number: 2011916414

Printed in the United States of America

WestBow Press rev. date: 10/04/2011

CONTENTS

Introduction vii

Chapter 1 –   What is a Dinosaur Anyway? 1

Chapter 2 –   Large, Slow Quadrupeds............................. 6

Chapter 3 –   In the Beginning 12

Chapter 4 –   The Rest of Moses' Writings 21

Chapter 5 –   Joshua to Solomon Behema / Behemoth
              All the Way..34

Chapter 6 –   The Prophets Speak of Behema / Behemoth..........42

Chapter 7 –   Moses' Staff...50

Chapter 8 –   Things With Wings.................................62

Chapter 9 –   Peter's Vision 73

Chapter 10 – The Rest of the New Testament......................83

Chapter 11 – The 'OWR' Connection 88

Chapter 12 – The Ox-Bullock, Unicorn and Other
              Odd Critters 104

Conclusion 111

Appendices

      Appendix I –   Uses of Behemoth / Behema 113

      Appendix II – Ninety-Five Theses: Evolution is a
                     Lie!—this section of this book is adapted
                     from the Internet Public Domain 127

      Appendix III – A poem honoring the countless Christian
                     martyrs through the ages..........................152

      Appendix IV – Other works by Glenn L. Wilson 154
                     Glenn's Short List of Recommended
                     Books and Organizations........................156

Appendix V –   The Biblical Basis for the Equality of
                Born-again People—specifically: Male /
                Female and so-called 'Races'......................157
Appendix VI – The Historical View of The Book of
                Revelation—particularly chapter 16.........165

Introduction

Dinosaurs have captured the imagination of mankind for all history. We see reconstructions of the monstrous reptiles in everything from comic books and movies to documentaries. In much of the popular media, the claim is almost universally made that these creatures lived many tens of millions of years ago. However, a growing number of qualified scientists and other researchers, such as myself—associated with creationist organizations have begun to explore the obvious contradiction between this claim of 'millions of years' of Earth's history and the account of a recently created Earth found in a straight forward reading of the Bible. The objective evidence from our natural world and universe; including an honest application of long accepted scientific Laws; support the Biblical account—hands down!

Several years ago, material from the Answers in Genesis organization prompted me to look into the issue myself. I could not have been prepared for what lay buried in the pages of the English translation of the Bible just waiting to be discovered! It would be hypocritical of me to say that I did the discovering. What really happened is that God did the revealing of this mystery to me. I think I now know what the wandering shepherd boy that found the Dead Sea Scrolls must have felt like. What the Lord has allowed me to find could—**and should**—completely revamp our understanding of this part of man's history! Like that boy; I do not have sufficient skill to probe this mystery completely—but I can and will tell the world what the Lord has allowed me to uncover. Then people who have a deeper understanding of the Hebrew language and culture will no doubt discover much more.

The only reason they didn't make the initial discovery is because God needed to give it to a person that He has worked with for many years to un-indoctrinate paradigms drilled into the brains of American kids. Specifically: The doctrines of: 'Molecules to man' evolution and 'Man never lived with dinosaurs' because the earth 'is billions of years old'—had to be smashed first. I thank the many creationist organizations that have demolished these mental barriers that had ruled my thinking for some twenty-seven years. Without their work; I too would likely have walked right by this tiny cave opening instead of going inside to find the hidden treasure that this world desperately needs.

I believe each person has a destiny and work to do for God. This must be mine—for the seemingly quite accidental sequence of events that took place seems to me to be best explained in the context of God's sovereign choice to reveal this information at this time in history. Many may be uncomfortable with a perspective that God reveals what He will when He will to whom He will—but this concept is critical to understanding much of the material contained in these pages. The Reverend John Robinson—the Pastor of the Pilgrims; stated in his farewell letter to those of his congregation first heading to the New World—that God was not finished revealing Truth from the Bible to man. He said this in firm belief that God would open the finished canon of Scripture to explain more mysteries than had thus far been revealed. It may be providential that I am his great grandson fourteen generations later.

If you are an Atheist or skeptic; you will not enjoy this book—for its pages will directly assault the underpinnings of your religion of evolution. If you are a Christian; you will thoroughly enjoy this book—it will strengthen your faith and give you new ammunition in the culture war that is gripping our nation and world as this world is prepared to receive King Jesus. More than ever, it is imperative that Christians be able to answer the question: Where do dinosaurs fit into the Bible? Many people who would like to believe in the God of the Bible and the Savior of the world: Jesus Christ—get stuck on this very question. Be assured: The answers were there all the time in the original language—they were just hidden from our eyes until God opened them at just the right time—now. Skeptics abound in our day and God silences His critics once more.

I will be writing from the perspective that the Earth is about six thousand (6000) years old. I will not attempt to prove it; but merely assume it to be true. Many others have done more than sufficient research to show the Earth cannot be billions of years old. If you have a problem with that; I suggest you settle the age of the Earth issue in your mind first and validate that creation is a better explanation of the evidence available for all to study and draw conclusions from. You can do a web search on the word 'Creationism' and find many sites that will give you many different views. You can compare those views and the evidence and then see which one makes the most sense. Another option is to look at Appendix II: The 95 Theses at the end of this book that show evolution is a lie. Then if you care to; come back and find out the truth about dinosaurs.

Each chapter will have a short summary of main points at the end—because some of this information gets a little complicated. It is the nature of this work to delve into some of the details of translation and transliteration from one language and culture to another.

CHAPTER ONE

What is a Dinosaur Anyway?

There it is!! A fully reconstructed Tyrannosaurus Rex complete with six inch teeth! It is poised over another large lizard that is about to become lunch. Off in the distance are pictures of huge beasts much larger than elephants—in a swamp; quietly watching the drama as they munch on seaweed. The world of the dinosaurs! Dog eat dog!—umm, I mean: Raptor eat raptor—with no mammals, no people, no modern looking plants. Many erupting volcanoes are seen and fierce looking flying lizards sail through the sky. Just how accurate is this scene? As with most issues today; it depends on whom you ask.

If you were to ask a believer in the Evolution Religion; he would tell you that what you are seeing is a fact! He would tell you that the Earth is known to be billions of years old and that dinosaurs ruled it for more than a hundred million years. The only problem is; were you to ask him if he actually saw any of it—he would have to say that he had not. What you have looked at is this person's pictorial representation of what they BELIEVE the evidence from fossils and other research reveals. What if the evolutionist had a PhD after their name and was a professor at a major college? Well, let's break the word professor down: The person is one who strongly or forcefully professes a view: A profess-or. If you profess faith in Jesus Christ—you are also a profess-or of Christianity! I am a profess-or of Creation based truth and of Bible Apologetics. In the centuries of old Rome, such Christians were called confessors—see the poem in Appendix III honoring the Christian martyrs of all ages.

If you were to ask a literal creationist; he would tell you that the Bible is true and all these imaginative displays are not true. He would tell you that the Bible tells us that on day six of the creation week; God made all creatures that live on land including the first man and

1

woman. He would then go on to say that even the great dinosaurs have always lived with man and all were at first peaceful plant eaters, even the T-rex!

Who is right? Are either of them right? After all you say, "I have read the Bible and I didn't read anything about dinosaurs in it!" If a word search for dinosaur is done on the English Bible versions in use today: The finding for dinosaurs is zero items located. Where are the dinosaurs if man has always lived with them? You are about to see that there are many dinosaurs mentioned throughout the Bible. I will show you that Esau domesticated them and Nehemiah rode them! You will see that Moses commanded Aaron to cast his staff before pharaoh and it turned into one! You will see that Old Testament Laws concerning clean and unclean creatures featured many dinosaurs or animals that likely were dinosaurs—and may have completely involved only dinosaurs! Surely you want to read on to see if such a claim could possibly be true.

What is a dinosaur anyway? In common usage today: A dinosaur is an English term used to describe any of a large number of reptiles that *may be* extinct (again depending on whom you ask and believe). They can range in size from smaller than chickens to larger than a school bus. I found tracks of a dinosaur that would have been about the size of a small dog, another track that measures barely three-quarters of an inch long and also a raptor's hooked claw imprint. They are the smallest privately held dinosaur footprints that I know of—and this is important for people to understand that some dinosaurs were very small; allowing Noah to easily have taken baby dinosaurs with him on the ark. Some dinosaurs walked on two legs, some on four, some swam and some flew. Some were definitely vegetarian and some seem to have eaten meat; either carrion or freshly hunted. The English word dinosaur encompasses them all; but that word is a rather recent entrant into human language. We must take a walk backward in time to see what dinosaurs were called by the people of long ago.

The word dinosaur was created in 1841—only a hundred seventy years ago! What were these animals called before that? Dragons! A dragon would be an adequate synonym for a large; potentially fierce reptile that lived on land or flew in the sky or swam in the sea. A dragon that lived in the sea would be called a sea monster or sea dragon. Many other authors have written about the various sea monster and dragon reports. Many reports are credible; some are obvious hoaxes. There are at least two video clips that I have seen of creatures that clearly appear to be large aquatic dinosaurs; one is of Champ (the Lake Champlain monster) and the other is of an unnamed creature in a lake on the west coast of the United States/Canada. Recently another video showing a brief surfacing of the head of a large aquatic animal in Loch Ness in the backdrop of a tourist boat about to go looking for Nessie! That is all I will say here and will leave further discussion to others. As for our purpose, we must go back much further into history.

The word 'dragons' is taken from the Greek word 'drakon' and was the accepted term from the mid-1800s all the way back to about 400 BC. The Babylonians were still around and in charge back then. They had just conquered the Israelite people of the remaining tribe of Judah and dragged them back to exile in Babylon. What were some of the other names for dinosaurs at the time the word dragon won out as the most common term?

One of the oldest languages known to man is the Hebrew language. Some believe it may be the original human language that was split into the various languages at the Tower of Babel. The topic of languages is another that others can handle better than I. Since we are only seeking information on big scary lizards, we will not delve into it. Knowing that Hebrew is one of the most ancient languages will suffice for our purpose.

Before we go further; the reader must clearly understand that I am not a Hebrew scholar—nor am I of Jewish decent. I cannot read Hebrew directly nor can I speak it very much. How then could I possibly state with such confidence what the Hebrew words mean? I told you that God has chosen to reveal this information not to the wise, but to the simple—me. He let me stumble on it and opened my mind to it. Had I been formally instructed in Hebrew; I would likely have missed it because I would have looked at these words the same way my teacher would have. Being a completely unlearned man in Hebrew—essentially teaching myself some of the language as I researched the Bible: I had no preconceptions. I simply went where I was led by the Holy Spirit. Let Him do the same for you!

This information is available to anyone who will look. The evidence is clear and compelling! It will not require blind faith, but simply looking up words that have been translated and transliterated into English by perhaps the greatest ancient language expert of the last century: Dr. James Strong, author of Strong's Exhaustive Concordance of the Bible (hereafter called Strong's). His work is the gold standard for most Christian seminaries even after 130 years.

Not every version of Dr. Strong's work will be used for this task—for there are many in print. The Strong's I will be using is probably one of the OLDEST and perhaps a copy of the ORIGINAL version! I found it at a garage sale for five bucks! It was published by Crusade Bible Publishers, Inc. This Strong's is so old that it does not even have a publish date or ISBN barcode. Also, there is no copyright statement. Dr. Strong apparently meant for all to have free access to his work—at least at that time. The copyright for more recent versions of Dr. Strong's work belongs to the various publishers. I will be using the Crusade version that has no copyright statement for my research in this work.

More than a century after Dr. Strong went home to hear; "Well, done! Good and faithful servant!"—his work lives on as a staple reference to all who love the Word of God. The only other tools you will need are a King James Bible (the work Dr. Strong originally made his reference for) and occasionally an English dictionary. I will be using the King James II Bible: Only the Words of God!—a special rendering of the King James Bible that my great grandmother left to me.

Summary of main points:

1) Evolution and Creation are opposite viewpoints—mixing the two cannot create a valid viewpoint—one is completely correct, the other is completely wrong
2) Dinosaurs were called Dragons in Greek and before that in Hebrew were called Behemoth, Behema, Tanniyn, etc.

3) Transliteration is choosing a word that conveys the essential idea when there is no know matching word in a language. Example: Behemoth is first called 'Cattle'

4) Strong's Exhaustive Concordance in its original and subsequent forms is the 'gold standard' for Bible scholars for the last approximately 125 years.

CHAPTER TWO

Large, Slow Quadrupeds

We start our search in the same place that God revealed it to me. Curiously, that place is not in the book of Genesis but the Book of Job at the 40th chapter and 15th verse where God says, "Behold now behemoth!—which I made with thee!" What in the world is a behemoth? In this conversation with Job; God is speaking about this real, visible creature to reveal something about Himself; an invisible Being. This animal was made for an important purpose and as we will soon see—and not just to impress Job.

The creature being described by God—for God is the One talking here—has the following physical characteristics: He is the chief, or greatest, of the ways of God!—in the Hebrew context that means: He is the biggest thing God made that lives or has ever lived on land. The fossil record shows that the biggest land dwelling animal would not be an elephant or mammoth; but rather some sort of sauropod like a Brachiosaurus. Behemoth has a large belly—strong legs—and a tail; but not just any tail! "He moveth his tail like a cedar!" continues God.

It is apparent that God is talking to Job about an animal that Job is very familiar with; since Job was a bit on the incapacitated side by this time in his ordeal. Job is there with his friends: There is no indication that he or his friends got up and went anywhere; least of all to a swamp—for it is revealed that the behemoth lives in the "covert of the reed and fens"—a swamp. There is also no indication that God transported the men millions of years back in time to see this critter. One reason they didn't go back millions of years—is because there were no millions of years to go back to! The millions of years idea is *an unprovable religious doctrine of the evolutionist faith!*

The straight forward reading of Scripture clearly indicates that God is referring to a real creature that Job could identify simply by this basic description! Yet Job did not have any museums bearing a fossilized skeleton of a Brachiosaurus; the creature that is larger than an elephant and would best fit God's description of a behemoth. It is preposterous to think that God projected an image for them to see and then talked about a creature that existed only in a vision. The best and most logical explanation is that Job would have seen a real, living behemoth to understand what God was saying to him! The behemoth would also have had to be a very important creature in these ancient cultures to have impressed Job so much.

Of course; what I have just said is not possible if evolutionists are correct in asserting that man and dinosaurs never lived together. Evolutionists interpret the evidence to fit their belief system—their religion—that the earth is billions of years old. All of the real uncontested evidence fits the young earth or literal creationist model {see Appendix II: The 95 Theses Proving Evolution is a Lie}. Therefore: Man living with dinosaurs like he does today with cows and horses is perfectly understandable and logical if creationists are correct in asserting that God made all the land animals on the same day He made man as God claims in Job 40:15.

Some have said the behemoth is an elephant or a hippopotamus. This assertion cannot be correct for remember: Neither of these animals is the largest (chief) land animal God has made. The Brachiosaurus is the largest from the fossil record. Neither elephants nor hippos have a tail that would remind a human writer, much less God, of a large cedar tree. Recall that it is God speaking in this section. Also; in Hebrew— the word rendered in English as "moveth" means "to hold erect without bending"—the way sauropods are now depicted since someone pointed out about twenty years ago that tail drag marks are never found with their fossilized footprints. Before that point was made, dinosaurs were shown dragging their tails on the ground behind them—like on the old Sinclair gas station signs. Now all dinosaurs are shown with tails held erect behind them—just as God said He made them.

Once again, man was wrong and God was right. Elephant tails hang down and hippo tails are really just a flap of skin and tissue. Remember;

God is the one talking in Job 40:15. I miss-speak from time to time; but not God. If He meant this animal had a tail the size and length of a tree held out off the ground behind him; this animal had a tail the size and length of a tree held out straight behind him!

The animal being described—if one lets any pre-existing paradigms of 'millions of years' and 'no man has ever seen a dinosaur' go would say this animal sounds like the dinosaur we call Brachiosaurus. The fossil evidence reveals these biggest of known creatures had large bellies, strong legs and a tree-like tail. It is likely they lived at least part of the time in the swamp or marsh. No other animal now alive or from the fossil record fits the description.

What on earth is a behemoth? If one looks in Strong's; it is word number 930 and is translated directly from the Hebrew as behemoth (Job 40:15) only this one time in the whole Bible. To catalog the entire Bible for people who wanted to find a particular verse; but could only recall a word from that verse: Dr. Strong broke the Bible down into individual English words and assigned each word a unique number. It took him about forty years! That number then is cross-referenced in a different section of the Strong's where that unique number has the actual Hebrew, Chaldean, Greek or Aramaic word translated or transliterated into the English word used in the scriptures.

So if you only remember behemoth, but don't know what verse it was in or what it means: You look in Strong's under the B's until you find it, identify the verse and can easily locate that verse in the Bible. One may also use the unique number in another way by turning to the Hebrew/Chaldean dictionary section in the back of the concordance and looking for the number. Right there beside the number is the word in its original language with the best definition we have and the English words that best translate or transliterate the word at the time Dr. Strong created his work. Got it now? Oh, ok—for those who just want the 'Reader's Digest' version; here it is.

Word 930 "behemoth (in form a plural of word 929, but really singular . . .) . . ." WHAT! Stop the world!! Behemoth is used once; but its plural form is word 929—behema. That word means, "Any large quadruped . . . often collectively." Behema is translated into the

8

following English words in the Old Testament; cattle, beast/beasts in the New Strong's and Strongest Strong's {two modern versions of Strong's}; but not in the Crusade published Strong's. In the older Strong's: Behema is translated only as beast/beasts and behemoth is rendered only as cattle except for the one time in Job when it is rendered directly as behemoth. Something that is best understood to be a Brachiosaurus is translated into English as cattle? In the newer versions of Strong's; behemoth/behema is translated as cattle 56 times and beast/beasts 134 times—a total of 190 times! In the OLD Crusade Strong's we find a different story.

In the OLD Strong's the word cattle (behemoth) is listed as word 930—58 times (possibly 60—the printing in this old book of mine is not clear in one section). In the old Strong's; behema is used as the word for beast/beasts and never for cattle. In the newer versions of Strong's, behema is claimed to be the word for cattle and beast/beasts. The two Hebrew words are similar but different enough to be easily distinguished by anyone as competent in the Hebrew language as Dr. Strong. Why then do the newer versions of Strong's say the word is behema? I do not know, but either they or Dr. Strong have it wrong and the only way to tell the difference is to have Hebrew scholars go back to the Masoretic Text and tell us which word is actually there. For the points made in this book; either behemoth or behema—being the Hebrew word for a Brachiosaurus or other large quadruped of similar nature—reveal that the Bible tells us that man has always lived with dinosaurs and when the context in which they occur is studied—it is very clear that man domesticated some of them and interacted with them in many other ways.

The Hebrew words behemoth and behema are used by God and Moses in Genesis Exodus-Numbers-Deuteronomy and exclusively by God in the book of Laws for the Jewish nation; Leviticus. The writers of Judges-Joshua-Samuel-Kings-Chronicles-Nehemiah-Ezra-Job-Psalms-Proverbs-Ecclisiastes use these words. The great prophets Isaiah-Jeremiah-Ezekiel all speak of behemoth/behema. No less than five other prophets also mention them. Both Jewish kings (David, Solomon) and a foreign king (Cyrus) use the words. These people—writing by God's inspiration—record various encounters with behemoth/behema over the course of several thousand years.

Appendix I contains all of the uses of Behemoth and Behema in the Old Testament if a person wants a detailed, concise tabulation. By the end of the first five books of the Bible; also called the books of Moses (Pentateuch)—56 phrases were spoken by God; 32 phrases spoken by Moses and 3 times other people use behema / behemoth with some phrases using the words multiple times in the same sentence for a total of 105 uses. It can be clearly demonstrated that behema and behemoth are NOT bovine animals; are used for labor and meat; in other cultures are used for ritual sex; are prized possessions taken in war—but most of all: WELL KNOWN and essentially integrated into Jewish and all other cultures from Egypt to Canaan! No wonder God tells Job to "Behold now behemoth . . ." with full expectation that Job knows exactly what animal He is talking about!

By the time the Old Testament ends; we find Behema/Behemoth used 20 more times as Behemoth and 70 more times as Behema AFTER the close of the Pentateuch—clearly behemoth and behema are: Domesticated and trainable, critical to a successful economy and next in line below man as special to God. About 4000 years of history have passed—God's view of these creatures has not changed; historical writers record consistent accounts and the world's most credible and reliable sources write the accounts! It is time for God to get the credit for His creation—including dinosaurs!

When I read the English translation of the Bible with my 20th century mind: A mind **conditioned to believe man and dinosaurs never lived together by public school 'science' teachers and books**—and I encounter the word 'cattle'—I naturally think of cows; not behemoth. Were I to read the word 'beast' or 'beasts' in English—I think of wild animals such as lions and tigers and bears (oh, my!)—not behema. Could substituting behemoth for cows and behema for wild animals make that much difference? Let us find out in the next chapter!

Summary of Main Points:

1) Behemoth is a sauropod such as a Brachiosaurus and / or Apatosaurus based on an unbiased analysis of the description God gives in Job 40:15

2) Behemoth was a living creature that Job was very familiar with, as were all the creatures God mentions from chapter 39 to 41 of the book of Job

3) Most people alive today have been conditioned to believe man and dinosaurs never lived together—this is a doctrine of the religion of evolution

4) Behema appears to be a general group term for a number of Behemoth—and there appears to have been a number of different types of Behemoth as well

5) Behema seems to be equivalent to our modern day English term Dinosaurs, Behemoth the equivalent of Sauropods, etc.

6) The English word 'moveth' means 'to hold erect without bending' behind the creature—now depicted for all dinosaurs in the last 20 years—at first, man drew dinosaurs dragging tail on the ground—God was right all along!

CHAPTER THREE

In the Beginning . . .

The first time the word behemoth appears is Genesis 1:24-26; "{24} And God said, 'Let the earth bring forth the living creature after its kind; cattle (behemoth) . . . {25} And God made the beast of the earth after its kind—and cattle (behemoth) after its kind . . . And God saw that it was good. {26} "And God said 'Let Us make man in Our image, after Our likeness: and let them have dominion over the fish of the sea, and over the fowl of the air, and over the cattle (behemoth) . . .' This year I turn fifty years old and have heard all my life from people who DO know how to read Hebrew that the word rendered cattle here meant domestic livestock such as cows, goats, sheep, oxen and such. Many new English translations of the Bible say 'domestic animals' at this point. I never knew the word was behemoth until I looked it up for myself in Strong's!

Let us read it again with behemoth substituted for cattle to see if it makes any difference. "And God said, 'Let the earth bring forth the living creature after its kind; behemoth, . . .'" Now do you think of livestock as we; 6000 years removed do? Do you not rather think of elephants? The only reason you do not think of a Brachiosaurus is because **you were conditioned in public school and/or college** by the prophets of the evolution religion **to believe these animals lived millions of years before man ever existed**!

According to OLD Strong's: The word rendered cattle here is the Hebrew word behemoth and by New Strong's it is behema. Either way: We are suddenly confronted with creatures we would call dinosaurs today—right in the first chapter of the Bible! As described in Job: The behemoth is a large quadruped that has a tail like a cedar tree held erect behind it. A cow, sheep, goat, ox, ass, horse, donkey, etc. do not have tails like this and there are other individual Hebrew words for each of these animals (if in fact those words are correct transliterations!). Often; the same writer selects behemoth or behema in the same sentence as these other animals! This is just the tip of the iceberg.

The rest of this book will reference only OLD Strong's identity of Hebrew words. My suspicion is that the New Strong's somehow got it wrong in rendering behemoth as behema. Again; the only way to prove it is to look at the actual Hebrew text to find out which word is there. It does not matter which word is there: One is either the plural of the other or is a grouping term that includes the other! All references then are sauropods if we let evolutionary preconceptions be set aside and take the description of behemoth found in Job at face value.

In Genesis 2:20 Adam gives names to the animals, "{2:20} And Adam gave names to all cattle (behemoth) . . ."—some claim Adam could not have named the multitudes of animals in the few hours since his creation. We now see that the Bible says he ONLY named the behemoth—he MAY have named the others or may have named them later. In bringing to Adam the greatest of His animal creations, God is clearly granting to Adam the right to name them all at some point, but not necessarily right then. God has a special purpose for these critters and so brings them to Adam for a name first. If skeptics would spend half as much time trying to believe God instead of trying to doubt Him—they could use their God given intelligence to make some truly worthwhile discoveries!

A new clue as to what order of animal a behemoth belongs to is found in Genesis 3:14 where God pronounces sentence on the serpent that deceived the woman into eating the forbidden fruit, "{3:14} And the Lord God said to the serpent, 'Because you have done this, you are cursed above all cattle (behemoth) . . . ' In Genesis 3:1 the serpent is identified as among the beasts of the field. The word rendered beasts here is the Hebrew word 'chay', meaning living thing. The word for serpent here is the Hebrew word 'nachash', from its characteristic hiss: A critter we would probably call a snake in our day. The animal mentioned could be the Anaconda—the only known snake in the world with an evident hip structure and non-functional withered legs. The Anaconda with legs may have looked very similar to the rendering of the evil lizard in Disney's <u>Monster's, Inc</u> movie. There are also credible eyewitness accounts from the early explorers of the Amazon rainforest of Anacondas growing to more than 80 feet in length, though the accepted proved record is somewhat over 20 feet.

Today; snakes have no legs—but here this serpent is called a type of behemoth or a beast of the field (or both?) and has its legs cursed off by God! A further effect of the curse is that the serpent's food would be changed from vegetarian, as all creatures were created to be, to dust (the Hebrew can also be rendered clay)—all land dwelling animals were created from the dust; therefore: Serpents will henceforth eat flesh. This agrees perfectly with what is observed today.

The first indication that man domesticated any animal at all comes from Genesis 4:20, "And Adah bare Jabal: he was the father of such as dwell in tents, and of such as have cattle (miqneh—acquired livestock—a term that DOES NOT preclude behema or behemoth as domesticated livestock)." Apparently man has always domesticated any animal over which he was given dominion. Later we will see that this included behemoth and behema—dinosaurs!

The next occurrence of behemoth / behema is the first reference to behema (Strong's word 929) found in Genesis 6:7, "And the Lord said, 'I will destroy man whom I have created from the face of the earth; both man and beast (behema) . . . . '" From the use of the word: I sense that perhaps we should understand behema may not exactly be the plural of behemoth, but rather a grouping term similar to the way we classify animals today according to Kingdom, Order, etc. In context, many uses of behemoth occur as both plural and singular like the English word moose—a single moose or a herd of moose. I propose the following understanding of the terms describing animals that we have encountered thus far.

Let us make a comparison between the way we would classify a brachiosaurus today with how the ancient Hebrews might have.

Genesis: Animal	Today's: Animal	Comments
Beasts (chay-living thing in which is the breath of life—can include air breathing flying and sea dwelling creatures) *except* man	Any life that belongs to the Animal Kingdom that breaths air no matter where found: air, land or sea—including man	Widest general term for all air breathing animals. Genesis makes it clear that man is not to be considered just one of the chay
Beasts (behema-large quadrupeds, a sub-division of the chay)—probably restricted to all dinosaurs	Elephants, hippos, giraffes, rhinos, lions, tigers, bears (oh my!), alligators, bison, water buffalo, Komodo dragons etc.	In English—a more general term applied to a number of large quadruped animals both mammal and reptile
Serpent (nachash-name Adam gave to this sub-type of behemoth &/or chay of the field).	Snakes of all varieties and sizes	Originally a type of behemoth &/or chay of the field until changed by God's curse in Gen 3:14

God's intention was to destroy man and beast (behema) as well as the other critters as a demonstration of the utter corruptness of sin. God—in His mercy—wanted to save representatives of the animals with the only man He deemed righteous in that generation. His family was also spared—though it is interesting that their spiritual condition is NOT specifically identified; only Noah's is. In Genesis 6:19-22 Noah is instructed to take dinosaurs on the Ark, "{19} And of every living thing of all flesh . . . shall you bring into the ark to keep them alive with you . . . {20} Of fowls; after their kind—and of cattle (behemoth); after their kind—and of creeping thing of the earth; after its kind . . . {22} Thus Noah did . . ." He took cattle: behemoth—with him! We see behemoth can be used as a plural by itself and need not have the word behema used when referring to more than one behemoth.

Another interesting fact arises; God is instructing Noah which animals will come to him to take on the ark. In so doing, God makes the first reference to clean and unclean beasts! Way back in Genesis 1:31 God proclaimed that all He had made was very good—so we would conclude that all beasts at that time were 'clean'. In Genesis 3:14, God curses the serpent (nachash); a behemoth or beast of the field in particular—so this group of critters known as nachash is now marred in God's sight for having been used of satan to deceive our first parents. Now as He speaks to Noah; God says for the first time that some animals are unclean (in the Hebrew literally: excrement) and some are clean (in the Hebrew: pure). In this proclamation; Creator God uses the word behema!

Genesis 7:2 says, "Of every clean beast (behema) you shall take to you by sevens . . . and of beasts (behema) that are not clean by two," Just to make sure we know this was not a misstatement, Genesis 7:8 repeats, "Of clean beasts (behema) and beasts (behema) that are not clean . . .". The point is further made by the use of beast (chay) and cattle (behemoth) in Genesis 7:14, " . . . and every beast (chay); after its kind—and all the cattle (behemoth); after their kind . . ." God is setting forth a subplot that will reach its culmination in the New Testament book of Acts more than 4000 years later! To discover this proof of a single Mind being the Author of all Scripture, read on.

Now the judgment Flood pours out and exterminates all land dwelling, air breathing life. Genesis 7:21 and 7:23 "{21} And all flesh died that moved upon the earth, both of fowl (things with wings), and of cattle (behemoth), and of beast (chay) . . . {23} And every living substance was destroyed . . . both man, and cattle (behemoth) . . ." The fossil record shows mass exterminations of all animals by water!—or as Answers in Genesis founder Ken Ham quips with his wonderful Australian accent, "If a world wide flood occurred; we would expect to see billions of dead things buried in sediments laid down by water all over the earth! What do we actually see?—billions of dead things buried in sedimentary rock that was laid down by water all over the earth!"

Now that God's righteous judgment has happened; it is time to bring Noah and his precious cargo to safety. Genesis 8:1 and 17-19, "{1} And God remembered Noah, and every living thing, and all the cattle (behemoth) . . . {17} Bring forth with you every living thing that is with you, of all flesh, both of fowl, and of cattle (behemoth) . . . that they may breed abundantly . . . {18} And Noah went forth . . . {19} Every beast (chay) . . . went forth out of the ark". Of all the land dwelling, air breathing animals on the ark; God only specifically takes note of the cattle (behemoth) and as this book progresses; we will see that God consistently takes particular note of these special creatures in the whole of the Old Testament.

In Genesis 8:20—Noah offers a sacrifice—and this offering sets the stage for all of Israelite worship of God by sacrifice. What animal is offered? Get ready for a shock, "{8:20} And Noah builded an altar unto the Lord—and took of every clean beast (behema) . . ." What is going on here? A paradigm change is in progress! God is pleased with the offering and promises never again to destroy the earth with a Flood and makes a covenant with both man and creature, "{9:9} And I, behold, I establish My covenant with you, and with your seed after you, {9:10} And with every living creature that is with you, of the fowl, of the cattle (behemoth), and of every beast (chay) of the earth."

Man did not just see dinosaurs on a daily basis in ancient times; but actually had domesticated them! Turn to Genesis 34:1-23. This is the account of the defiling of Dinah, the daughter of Jacob. Some of the sons of Jacob decide to get revenge on the man who had inflicted this horrible crime on their sister. They made a proposal to the him; saying they would consent to the inter-marriage if the men of the village would get circumcised; knowing that the men would be incapacitated for some time afterward. The deal is discussed and in Genesis 34:23 by the man who had committed the crime tells his fellows, "{34:23} Shall not their cattle (miqneh-acquired livestock) . . . and every beast (behema) of theirs be ours?" The word cattle here is the Hebrew word that means acquired livestock. This reference to domesticated livestock and behema is far from unique.

Turn to Genesis 36:6. This is the passage where Jacob and Esau are going to part company because the land cannot continue to provide for all the animals they had. Esau tells his brother that he is heading for a new land and Jacob can have this one. In the verse above; it states that Esau gathered "all his cattle (miqneh—acquired livestock), and all his beasts (behema) . . ." and headed out. Again we find cattle and beasts in the same phrase.

The same Hebrew word is often rendered as different English words many times in the Bible. The English word cattle that means acquired domesticated livestock is 4735 in Strong's and is spelled miqneh. The word rendered beasts is behema! So Esau gathered all his acquired domesticated livestock such as sheep, goats, cows, elephants, etc. and all his large quadrupeds such as Brachiosaurs; Triceratops, Stegosaurs, etc. and headed out. Esau had domesticated behema; not just sheep and goats! Perhaps the fantasy movie by Disney™ called Dinotopia™ was not such a fantasy after all—at least in terms of domesticating dinosaurs {the rest of it is complete bunk in my opinion}!

If you need more convincing; turn to Genesis 47. Joseph has risen to power and has consolidated all the wealth of the land under Pharaoh due to the terrible famine. All the people had been selling everything they owned to get enough food to survive. The large quadrupeds apparently are extremely valuable because they are the last animals the people part with.

Throughout the chapter the people are giving up their other cattle (miqneh–acquired livestock) identified in verse 17 as horses, flocks, herds, and asses. This allowed them to live almost the entire year; but as that year ended and the famine continued—the people returned to sell their own bodies saying to Joseph, " . . . my lord also has our herds (miqneh–acquired livestock) of cattle (behema), there is not anything left . . . . but our bodies and our lands." The word 'herds' here is the word that just one verse earlier was rendered as the English word cattle! The message conveyed appears to be, "You already got all our smaller cattle; then got our large quadrupeds—all that is left is ourselves and land." When in extremis; people part with belongings in order of importance and value. Clearly; behema were highly valued animals ranked right behind selling oneself into slavery and becoming a non–land owner.

Another indication of the value of behema and behemoth is that placed on these animals by God is in Numbers 3:12&13. God takes the Levites to Himself as a memorial to the plague of death on the first born of Egypt, both man and beast (behema). Then in Numbers 3:41 God decrees that He will take the cattle (behemoth) of the Levites rather than the cattle (behemoth) of the Israelites as His prized possession. Clearly, behemoth are prized animals in the economy of God. This idea is underscored in Numbers 18:15 where God instructs Moses that the firstlings of man or the unclean beasts (behema) shall be redeemed.

God specifically ties the welfare of behema to that of his chosen people! In Numbers 20:8 Moses is to speak to the rock to " . . . bring forth to them water out of the rock: so you shall give the congregation and their beasts (behema) drink." The only animals God mentions, of the millions they no doubt had, are behema. Need more proof? Turn to Jonah 4:11—here is the very famous passage where God expresses His concern for the heathen in Nineveh, "And should I not spare Nineveh, that great city, wherein are more than six-score thousand persons . . . . and also much cattle (behemoth)."

Further evidence is offered in the way behema are treated in the battle between Midian and Israel in Numbers 31 and specifically verse 11. The victorious Israelites bring back their " . . . prey, both of men and of beasts (behema)". Of the captive humans, only the young virgin girls are saved alive—but all of the behema are saved alive! In verses 26-30; God instructs Moses as to how to divide the spoil taken—with half of the behema being given to God's set aside tribe; the Levites, " . . . which keep the tabernacle." The obvious implication is that these behema would be put to use pulling the carts that bore God's tabernacle and/or to be used erecting it {except for those items specifically to be carried by men}! After all; there were many metal parts to the tabernacle that would have been very heavy and would have logically been loaded on carts. The Levites personal belongings would need transport as well.

The book of Numbers final use of the word behema occurs in Chapter 35:3. God has set aside cities for the Levites to live in and, " . . . for their cattle (behemoth), ... and for all their beasts (miqneh-acquired livestock)". Again we see God's specific mention of provision for the behemoth. These creatures must be very special in the sight of God to receive so many references by Him and so much concern for their well being. Since this is so; would God really have allowed them to go extinct?

Earlier this century, Dr. Kent Hovind tells of an expedition to the vast swamps of the Congo region of Africa. Natives were shown pictures of animals from a coloring book. They recognized cows, goats and chickens—but not horses. Then the page was turned to a supposedly 'pre-historic' and 'extinct' creature: Apatosaurus. The natives excitedly pointed to the picture, loudly saying, 'Kongo-mato! Kongo-mato! Yes! We know him. He lives in the swamp." The natives did not dare disturb him as he fed among the swamp plants—for he would upset their canoe and drown them! God said to Job that behemoth lives 'in the covert of the reeds and fens.'—a swamp. Job did not attempt to ask God, "What is a behemoth?"—but knew exactly what animal God was talking about . . . . hmmmmm. It seems clear that it is the evolutionist religion of 'man never seeing or living with dinosaurs' that is in serious error.

Summary of main points:

1) Noah took dinosaurs on the Ark with him—and released them after the Flood—there could still be dinosaurs alive today—many dragon legends and sea monster reports may be based on fact!

2) The animal sacrifice system eventually adopted by the Jewish nation was originally a dinosaur sacrifice, for Noah offered a clean behema!

3) Clean and unclean animals as a concept was introduced with Noah, the animals labled clean and unclean were ONLY behema—dinosaurs!

CHAPTER FOUR

The Rest of Moses' Writings

Now let us move to Exodus and the slavery of the Israelites in Egypt. Moses has just been commissioned by God at the burning bush to come free them and he has had the initial encounters with Pharaoh's magicians. A few chapters from now; we will take a look at that specific scene out of this whole narrative to see if maybe there was more to it than just a snake fight.

The plagues begin to take their toll and we see a glaring contradiction in the Bible—in the English language. As I state throughout this work: The Bible is inerrant in its original language as understood by the culture of the time. Fallible men then translated and transliterated the Holy Scripture into many languages—sometimes they did quite well; sometimes, not so much.

Did you know that the New International Version (NIV)— America's most popular version when it first came out—omitted several sections of Scripture found in the King James Bible? One verse left out is the warning by Jesus that He is about to return in Revelation 16:15!—an error that has since been corrected in most NIVs. Another issue with the NIV is that in many places where the original language uses King Jesus' title name: Lord Jesus Christ—the NIV simply uses Jesus. Why? The full Name is there—why not use it? When He returns, it will be as King—not elected President or majority vote Prime Minister. Many Americans will have some significant adjusting to do—learning how to behave before the Ultimate King—the Lord Jesus Christ; their version of the bible having not impressed on them sufficiently His universal Kingship as Lord over ALL the earth. Remember what He said as He departed, "All authority has been given unto Me . . . ."

At any rate, in the eighth chapter of Exodus; the plague of lice comes upon man and beast (behema). It is obvious that the Egyptians had large numbers of domesticated behema! Maybe that is how they built the pyramids! I bet you could haul those big bricks anywhere you wanted if you hooked up twelve Brachiosaurs to it!

The beasts of the Egyptians in this verse were not cattle such as sheep and goats, because those 'cattle' get the next plague in Exodus 9 and Moses takes extra space in that chapter to tell us that the cattle involved in Exodus 9 were horses, asses, sheep, etc. The word cattle used in chapter 9 means 'acquired livestock'—but apparently in that specific use does not include behema / behemoth; some of which will die in the next plague. In the ninth chapter; the plague of the grievous murrain was upon all the cattle and causes ALL the cattle to die. Important point; ALL the cattle died, except the cattle of the Israelites in Goshen. Then—sequentially—comes the plague of hail.

God tells the Egyptians to get their remaining cattle (miqneh-acquired livestock) out of the field to save them from the hail. Wait a minute! Did not the Bible just say that all the cattle had died? Yes! Most analysts here say that not all the cattle had been killed in chapter nine, just the local ones; the ones in the field had not been affected. When will we stop making excuses for the Bible and just look at what it actually says in the original language?! What the Scripture actually says is: All the acquired livestock of the apparently non-behemoth / behema kinds were killed by the grievous murrain. Now the remaining cattle (miqneh) in the field will be killed by the hail. If you read the passage in the Hebrew, the apparent contradiction disappears.

God goes on to identify which cattle (miqneh) He is talking about. Exodus 9:19 says, " . . . every man and beast (behema) which shall be found in the field . . . ." will be killed by the coming plague. The Egyptians had humans taking care of their behema in the field! Man with dinosaurs: Domesticated dinosaurs! Since the Bible is TRUE—the evolution religious dogma of 'no man with dinosaurs' is FALSE!

Think about it, there would be many uses for such large animals; heck, you could finish the 'back forty' in a hurry with a Brachiosaurus pulling the plow! If you were raising the behema for meat; think of all the hamburgers you could make out of just one! It wouldn't be that hard to tame them; elephants have chains placed around their feet as babies. Soon they learn that they cannot get away. As adults, the chain is replaced with a small rope and isn't even hooked to anything—the elephant doesn't try to run away because it feels the rope and believes it is still captive by the chain it struggled in vain against as a baby. Further, a zookeeper told me that elephants will not venture into a depression that is deeper than their trunk can touch the bottom of. If behema were similarly able to be corralled, they would not even try to escape.

Now after seeing many plagues announced by Moses take place; many Egyptians apparently heeded the warning and moved their behema into a hail-proof shelter. We know this because the final plague of the death of the first born also fell on the firstborn of the beasts (behema). Then we see that the Israelites also had domesticated behema; because the plague would not fall on their beasts. When the final plague came, it struck all the firstborn including all the cattle (behemoth) according to Exodus 12:29. The Israelite people leave Egypt; taking with them all their cattle (miqneh-acquired livestock) of all types, including their domesticated behema / behemoth.

Now here is a real shocker! In Exodus 13, God tells the Israelites that the first born of every man and beast (behema) belongs to Him! God is not asking for the first born of sheep, goats, horses, etc. but the first born of the behema! Then the matter gets a little murky when the English translation says that God tells the Israelites to break the neck of an unredeemed first born male ass. The word ass (2543-chamowr) is not distinct but rather means "dun red"—there is no way to know if this really is the English ass or not; but in context here, God identifies it as a type of behema. Therefore it would seem that it must be some sub-type of critter that would be considered under the grouping behema since God did not give further clarification.

The next time the word behema shows up is when God gives the instruction regarding man and beast entering onto the Mount Sinai. God says that if a man or beast (behema) comes onto the mount, it is to be killed. God then tells the Israelites to observe the Sabbath by refraining any man or cattle (behemoth) from working. There can be NO legitimate doubt that these animals were domesticated.

At least two laws dictated to Moses by God involved behema / behemoth. The first was how to handle the case of an animal such as an ass, ox or any beast (behema) that died while in another person's care. The other law involved a man lying with a beast (behema) as with a woman; that man was too corrupt to be allowed to live. These two uses of the word behema conclude the uses in the book of Exodus.

The book of Leviticus picks right up in chapter one verse two, this time speaking about offering a behemoth as a sacrifice! It should be noted that ALL times behemoth or behema is used in Leviticus—it is God speaking! The offering may be of the cattle (behemoth), the herd (baqar-beeve/ox), or the flock. The 'cattle'—behemoth in its plural understanding—is separated from all other lesser creatures. The latter two terms—herd and flock—always refer to smaller domesticated animals such as oxen or sheep / goats in the rest of the Bible.

In the King James Bible at this verse, the fallible human translators add a word—'even'—that is not in the original language. You know this because the word is in italics, meaning it is added in an attempt to make the English clearer. Unfortunately, the true meaning is further obscured by this uninspired choice of words that results in grouping cattle and herd into a single category when read by an English reader—when that is not the meaning intended. In the original Hebrew, God calls out three distinct categories: cattle (behemoth), herd, or flock. Just because this did not make sense in 1611, does not mean it does not make sense in the original language as understood by the original audience. Also, it should give you a desire to know God's Word and ONLY God's Word. So here is a shameless plug for another of my works: The King James II Bible—Only the Words of God!—see how to get one in Appendix IV in the back of this book. All funds over production costs of the KJII Bible will go to support missionaries around the world—so even if you do not like this book; please spread the word about KJII.

To give you another example of how a single word translated into two different English words can make a huge difference, consider Revelation 18:4 in the Geneva Bible versus the 1611 King James Bible. The Geneva Bible came first and was the Bible used by the Pilgrims. In Revelation 18:4—the command by God to His people to leave Great Babylon reads, "Go out of her, My people . . .". In the King James it reads, "Come out of her, My people . . ." The pilgrims—of which my great grandfather fourteen generations ago was their pastor—gave up everything: Land, title, influence, security, etc—because they were Separatists, not Puritans. Puritans wanted to purify the Church of England from within it, Separatists believed the Church of England was the next great manifestation of satanic corruption—and that it could not be fixed.

They read Revelation 18:4 as a command to leave England—and obeyed! As a result, they embarked the Mayflower and settled America. So resolute were they to obey God that even after that first winter where about half of the settlers died, when Mayflower set sail to go back to England—NONE of the settlers went with her. They did send a letter back to my great grandfather asking if maybe they had misinterpreted God's Will; because so many of their number had died. Their pastor's answer can be paraphrased as, "God has saved alive sufficient to accomplish what He would in this new land." They were to stay. Stay they did.

The King James Bible was not widely used until well after the Pilgrims had already left. Even if it had been available—these folks would not have used it since it was this same King James that had persecuted them so severely from 1603 to 1620! One single word translated differently may have been responsible for the founding of the America we know today! Yes, Jamestown was already in existence, but as a colony was going nowhere—and most of the major governing principles of the America we know—as well as the Liberty movement itself—came out of the Plimoth (yes, that is the original spelling) colony area which became Boston . . . . but I digress.

The next time behemoth appears is again as the English word cattle; but in reference to a dead animal. The Israelites were not to touch the carcase (a rotted, flabby thing) of only the unclean types of chay (living thing). This distinction further tells us that Moses is not talking about oxen, sheep, goats, pigs, etc. All of these animals are clean. The animal is not declared unclean simply because it is dead or even because it is rotted. The animal is unclean because it is a certain type of behema! Remember back to the passage of Noah? Noah was to take clean behema by sevens and unclean by twos. It would seem that a great deal of research into the actual Hebrew language needs to be done by people much smarter than me.

We now move on to a very interesting chapter in Leviticus; chapter eleven. Most people just skip Leviticus altogether or use it as a sleeping aid—but this book contains the most detailed listings of dinosaurs in the Bible! This chapter contains the list of animals that God tells Moses are clean and unclean. The word behema figures large in this chapter. It is used from verse 3 to 8 as a grouping term for the sub-lists in those verses! This point is very important; because the English words chosen for the Hebrew words are mostly transliterations. In other words; the English specific animal is chosen because it—today has (or better, in 1611 had) the characteristic described by the Hebrew word. The result is a confusing combination of animals; many of which are not large quadrupeds in English as we understand behema to mean to this point. Whole sections of the list are supposed to be composed of <u>only</u> large quadrupeds.

In Leviticus 11:2; God sets the tone for verses 3 to 8 with the statement rendered in English, "Speak to the children of Israel, saying, 'These are the beasts (chay) which you shall eat among all the beasts (behema) that are on the earth." The next five verses therefore must be understood to be talking about these large quadrupeds called behema. God gives physical descriptions of these animals so that the Israelites will not sin against Him by eating or touching an unclean beast (behema). Again we go back to Noah. The only unclean beasts (chay) that Noah brought on the Ark were certain unclean behema.

If we properly understand the command of God consistent with instructions to Noah; we will discover that many of the transliterated critters given English names really do not fit at all! Also; many troublesome 'apparent contradictions' are easily cleared up. Verse three underscores that God is defining the clean beasts (behema) as only the ones that ' . . . part the hoof and are cloven footed, chews the cud'—in English the connecting word 'and' is inserted after the word 'footed' in the King James Bible—it is not in the original text. If a behema 'divides the hoof and is clovenfooted, cheweth the cud': It may be eaten. Since God is only prohibiting the eating of certain types of behema: All of the other chay—living creatures that breathe air—may be eaten, as ALL of them are clean—even sea monsters may be eaten. Another passage in Scripture covered later in this book identifies that 'sea monsters' less than Leviathan apparently were caught and eaten!

This list of clean behema begins with the transliterated English animal 'coney'. The Hebrew simply means 'to conceal'. The modern day assignment of coney or rock-rabbit does not agree with the designation of behema in verses two and three! Any large quadruped that has the ability to change color to match its surroundings—like the chameleon does in our day—would be a better fit. A large dinosaur that has the ability to change color would be the most logical choice.

Next is the hare. Again; a look at the Hebrew word reveals that it is of uncertain derivation and Strong's is simply taking a guess. A hare does not agree with the behema designation of verses two and three. Logic forces us to conclude that some kind of behema that chews the cud but does not have a divided hoof is truly the animal that is to be avoided for food and when dead—must not be touched.

The next animal declared unclean is rendered 'swine' in English. It is transliterated as well! The word means 'to inclose' and Strong's simply takes a shot at what it means, calling it a swine or pig. Even the largest pig on the planet cannot come close to qualifying as a behema as clearly understood to this point. Rather; all pigs would have been included under the classification of either herd (ox or beeve) or flock (sheep or goat) sized animals. Whatever this animal really is; we only know that it has a divided hoof but doesn't chew the cud and it was a behema. In our day, many Jewish persons avoid pork because of this verse—when this restriction in diet may not be indicated according to my research.

The next series of verses in Leviticus 11; verses 9-12, deal with living things that live in the waters. This is pretty simple, all that have fins and scales may be eaten.

Now God deals with fowls in verses 13-25. The Hebrew word for fowl is not the same as bird. This word can mean bird but can also refer to anything that has wings and /or flies. This passage is covered in more detail in a later chapter—for now; it is sufficient to say that nearly all of the flying or winged creatures specifically identified by an English name are transliterated.

Leviticus 11:26 returns the discussion to land dwelling behema with the statement, " . . . of every beast (behema) which divides the hoof and is not clovenfooted, nor chews the cud, are unclean to you . . ." God picks up with unclean animals among the beasts (chay-living things) with the final statement that those having four paws (not necessarily like today's tiger or wolf)—these renderings will need further examination by those more expert in Hebrew than I am.

God then addresses the subject of smaller animals that swarm and wiggle. Most of these animals are also transliterated and could just as easily be more consistently named as different types of reptiles. This also will be covered in a future section.

God once again returns to discuss behema in verse 39 where He says that if a behema that normally could be eaten dies of itself; it may not be eaten and may not even be touched without incurring uncleanness. If someone chooses to eat of the dead behema; that person is unclean and must also wash their clothes. Apparently these large quadrupeds were bred for both labor and food. I wonder if they tasted like chicken?

The last mention of behema in Leviticus is in the next to last verse of the chapter where the laws are summed up and God reaffirms that He meant behema to be the main part—if not exclusive whole—of the list. Verse 46, "This is the law of the beasts (behema), of the fowls (things with wings), and of every living creature (chay) that moves in the waters, and of every creature that creeps (the small swarming or wiggling things)."

In Genesis, Exodus and Leviticus alone, the word behemoth is used by God and Moses no less than 20 times as the English word cattle—and behema is used 47 times as the English word beast / beasts. That is a total of 67 times of the 190 occurrences of either beast or cattle. If you add in Numbers and Deuteronomy, the tally grows for a total of 105 uses of behema / behemoth out of 190 total occurrences. Clearly God and Moses meant to convey that they were speaking about large quadrupeds that best fit a sauropod description and not what 20th century man would consider cattle or beasts.

Let us move on to the book of Deuteronomy. Would you believe that 19 of 21 times the English words beast / beasts or cattle are used in this book it is the word behema or behemoth? Count for yourself in any version of Strong's. The first uses are in Deuteronomy 2:35 and 3:7 stating what animals were taken after the Israelites defeated Sihon and Og; kings of the Amorites. Again, the great value of behema / behemoth is evident in that the absolute monarchs of neighboring kingdoms had them.

If behema were so valuable to the Israelites, why don't we have any carvings or statues of them? It is well known that the Israelites were not to make any graven images of any created thing, right? No! God specifically prohibits the making of a few special classes of animal in Deuteronomy 4:16&17, "Less you corrupt yourselves, and make you a graven image, the similitude of any figure . . . . the likeness of any beast (behema) that is on the earth, the likeness of any winged fowl that flieth in the air." Of all the animals that man would tend to worship instead of God; behema and flying dragons are ones that would inspire man to do so—and neighboring cultures apparently were having ritual sex with behema in their religious ceremonies. These critters really must have been quite impressive. This also would explain why when Solomon made graven images of oxen (baqar) as the base of the bronze sea for the Temple—God did not chasten him for doing so!—but showed up in an unmistakable way at the dedication ceremony. Oxen (baqar) must not be behema.

Some of you still are having a tough time with this new paradigm of man domesticating dinosaurs. That is okay; old thought patterns die hard. More proof is found in Deuteronomy 5:14, "But the seventh day is the Sabbath of the Lord your God; in it you shall not do any work, you, nor your son, nor . . . etc. etc. . . . nor your ox, nor your ass, nor any of your cattle (behemoth) . . . ."! Obviously a behemoth is not an ox or ass, and as a large quadruped, it must be bigger than the ox. An elephant qualifies in general as a large quadruped. A brachiosaurus would, too. The brachiosaurus fits the description found in Job 40:15 while the elephant does not.

Chapter 7 of Deuteronomy contains the blessings the Israelites will enjoy if they obey God when they possess the land. In this culture, large families were considered a sign that God was blessing or 'with' a man or tribe. If one was barren, it was often a source of shame. God again shows the value of the behema by specifically saying that, " . . . there shall not be male or female barren among you (humans), or among your cattle (behemoth)." The importance of behemoth to the success of the Israelite economy is underscored in chapter 11:13-15 " . . . if you shall hearken diligently to My commandments . . . I will send grass in your fields for thy cattle (behemoth), that you may eat and be full." Now we also know what behemoth eat: grass—just like God said to Job.

The self purging of evil that might arise in Israel is a major topic in the Old Testament. If a city were to rebel against the Lord, it faced complete extermination of all its people—and all its behemoth! Deuteronomy 13:12-16, "If you hear-say in one of your cities . . . the children of Belial (the devil) . . . have withdrawn the inhabitants of their city, saying, 'Let us go and serve other gods' . . . Then shall you enquire . . . and, behold!—if it be truth . . . . You shall surely smite the inhabitants of that city with the edge of the sword, destroying it utterly, and all that is therein, all the cattle (behemoth) thereof . . . and you shall gather all the spoil of it into the midst of the street thereof and shall burn with fire the city . . . it shall not be built again." The behemoth were even to be destroyed if a city turned from God; again, these creatures are given special attention.

The subject of transliteration versus translation between languages becomes very important when apparent contradictions appear. When passages occur that seem completely against an understanding that holds true elsewhere or even throughout the rest of Scripture—some rules must be remembered! First—the Bible is 100% accurate IN ITS ORIGINAL LANGUAGES and as understood IN CONTEXT OF THAT CULTURE. English is a TRANSLATION from the original languages and is a decidedly different culture—misunderstandings are bound to occur that God may or may not choose to correct in some way. He is choosing to correct the record concerning dinosaurs in this work.

Therefore: God is right and consistent—even if we humans cannot figure out what He is saying for a time. Second—Scripture does not contradict Scripture! Therefore; even if this interpretation which understands behema and behemoth to be dinosaurs finds ANY point in Scripture that proves the premise false—it is my premise or part of it that is false; not Scripture! Armed with these two rules; we will look at an apparent contradiction and offer a possible explanation. It may well be that Hebrew scholars will be better able to explain it than I.

Translation between languages is not a perfect science. One missionary to an isolated tribe discovered that they had no word in their language for heart. Yet he needed to tell them that they desperately needed to accept Jesus into their hearts to be saved. The only solution was to use the symbol closest to the meaning the missionary wanted to communicate. This tribe had a hand motion that symbolized being overcome or choked up with emotion—moving the hand to the throat. In America we would respond to such a gesture by executing a Heimlich maneuver! The missionary was able to get the salvation message across by transliterating the best he could. God knows the heart and knows that these people have been choked up with emotion by the gift of forgiveness of sins through Jesus.

Deuteronomy 14:4-6 states, "These are the beasts (behema) that you shall eat: The ox, the sheep, and the goat, the hart, and the roebuck, and the fallow deer, and the wild goat, and the pygarg and the wild ox, and the chamois. And every beast (behema) that parts the hoof, and cleaveth the cleft into two claws, and chews the cud among the beasts (behema) . . . ." To leave this passage out would be to tell a half truth— and you honored me by trusting me to tell you the whole truth.

In Hebrew culture and language—it appears to have been common practice to not name a particular animal; but rather to describe its unique features and use that characteristic as it's name. For a rough parallel: Think of the scene in the movie <u>Dances with Wolves</u> where Kevin Costner tries to tell the Indians that he had spotted a large herd of buffalo or ta-tanka—he could only act out the animal to overcome the language barrier. The word ox in this passage is not the Hebrew baqar but rather showr— meaning 'a traveler'. Showr is the word transliterated into the English word ox throughout much of the Old Testament. The word sheep here is the Hebrew keseb meaning 'a young sheep' according to Strong's (remember, even Dr. Strong was not perfect in language translation and may have not had perfect understanding in all words) but derived from another word meaning 'to butt' as in a ram or goat. Keseb is not the usual word for sheep; tseown is the usual word and it means 'to migrate'. Tseown is the word used for the animal that Abel sacrificed. It is a pretty definite word, much more so than keseb. The word rendered goat above is the Hebrew word ez and means 'male or female goat' but is derived from another word that means 'be strong or prevail'. The writer—in the ancient Hebrew culture—has chosen descriptions that his audience would know; though we in modern times do not. We can be sure Scripture does not contradict Scripture—so this entire list of animals ARE types of behema—though the English transliterations would not be dinosaurs or sauropods.

Most importantly, NO doctrines of Christianity are affected by our inability to fully understand these critters in the English language. A doctrine is a concept that if removed from a belief system—fundamentally changes that belief system. For instance; take the doctrine of the religion of evolution that demands dinosaurs never lived with man. If it can be shown that this dogma is false (and this belief is shown to be false in this book)—the religion of evolution is also false! Man must NEVER have interacted with dinosaurs for the religion of evolution to be true.

In Christianity; an example of a doctrine is the bodily resurrection of Christ—if Christ never rose from the dead; Christian faith is falsified! All these animals—whatever they really were—whether dinosaur or mammals or whatever; are associated with the Old Testament concepts of clean / unclean and the Jewish sacrificial system of atonement. For the Christian; this system is done away with by the New Testament sacrifice of Christ for sins! The only religious system that could be fatally threatened by the ideas in this book is the religion of evolution—which is falsified if man and dinosaur lived together!

I told you I am not a Hebrew scholar. All I am doing is relating information that you can look up yourself in Strong's. You must do your own research to decide what has happened in this passage. As for me, I believe these critters are behema because the Scripture says they are and there is considerable uncertainty about many if not most of the animals named with specific English words in the Old Testament. One Hebrew professor at Columbia International University in Columbia, SC told me that only about forty percent of the animal references in the Old Testament are clearly known to be a certain animal (I would argue much less than 40%). He said the rest were open to interpretation. Even if it were 0%—no doctrine of Christianity is affected. The Old Testament exists to give us historical context for the New Testament! I plan to ask Moses when I get to heaven—since he wrote this!

Let us move on. The final mentions of behema in Deuteronomy involve the blessings of obeying God in fertility of all their agricultural efforts and the curses of disobeying God in the sterility of their women and their behemoth. One of those curses is particularly interesting; turn to Deuteronomy 28:26. If the people turn from God, He will allow them to be defeated in battle " . . . and your carcasses shall be meat to all the fowls of the air and to the beasts (behema) of the earth . . . ." Apparently some behema are meat eaters or become meat eaters under certain circumstances. Elephants have never been documented to eat meat so far as I know. Hippos do eat meat occasionally, but do not fit Job 40:15 in the tail or size department—and I really have a hard time imagining hippos coming out of their normal habitat and foraging on corpses after a battle—in semi-mountainous terrain—or in desert areas. The eating of dead bodies also throws doubt on the English transliterations of 'birds' in Leviticus 11. This will be explored in a later chapter.

In Moses' final song, found in Deuteronomy 32—contains at verse 24 these words of God that indicate some behema may be or may become meat eaters; " . . . I will also send the teeth of beasts (behema) upon them . . ." Moses' writings are finished and more than half of the uses of behema / behemoth have occurred.

Summary of main points:

1) The majority of uses of the words behema and behemoth are by God and Moses in the Old Testament
2) The Levitical Laws regarding clean and unclean animals involved ONLY types of behema—i.e. dinosaurs
3) God takes the first born of behema as a substitute for the firstborn of man—behema and behemoth receive special attention throughout the Old Testament
4) Dinosaurs could be and were eaten!—they would have been raised for food and labor just like any other domesticated animal
5) Some types of behema eat meat, specifically human corpses under certain circumstances
6) Many cultures were familiar with behema and behemoth

CHAPTER FIVE

Joshua to Solomon
Behema / Behemoth All the Way

In the book of Joshua, 4 of 7 references to the English word cattle are the word behemoth—with the other 3 references being miqneh-acquired livestock. The first occurrence is in Chapter 8 as the Lord commands Joshua to take the city of Ai. The Israelites are to do to Ai what they did to Jericho except that this time they may take the spoil "and the cattle (behemoth) . . ." Ai appears to have been located up in the hill country, perhaps even the low mountains of what is today the country of Israel. Behemoth of the sort mentioned in Job seemed to live in the swamp or marsh. As stated before; I believe the word behemoth encompasses many different types of large quadrupeds, some that lived in the swamp; others that would tolerate living in the hill country. The other references of behemoth in Joshua repeat previously examined ideas and may be examined in more detail in Appendix I.

There is only one time the word behema is used in the book of Judges. It is found at Judges 20:48. The tribe of Benjamin had given shelter to some men who had brutally raped and murdered the concubine of a traveling Levite after demanding to have the Levite surrendered to them for a homosexual orgy. This crime was made known to the other tribes. Israel collectively realized that they were beginning to reap the curses God had said would come on them for turning from Him to other gods (sound familiar America?). They repented and sought the Lord for direction (we should, too—America!).

God directed them to muster an army and destroy these wicked persons. The tribe of Benjamin would not give them up for some reason and so the other tribes fought against the entire tribe of Benjamin. Once the Benjamites had been defeated; the rest of the army carried out God's directive by exterminating all of the Benjamite cities " . . .

with the edge of the sword, as well the men of every city, as the beast (behema) . . ." The tribe of Benjamin was reduced to only 600 men when once they had been well over 100,000 men, a very high price to pay for protecting the wicked murderers (is America listening?).

There is also one occurrence of behema in the books of 1 and 2 Samuel. It is found in 1 Samuel 17:44 as part of the curse Goliath pronounced on David, "Come to me and I will give your flesh to the fowls of the air, and to the beasts (behema) of the field." Again we have evidence that some behema ate meat at least part of the time. The eating of meat pretty much rules out elephants as being the behema Goliath was referring to.

In 1 and 2 Kings the word behema occurs four times. The first is 1 Kings 4:33 where King Solomon's achievements are being recorded, "And he spoke three thousand proverbs . . . . And he spoke of trees . . . . he spoke also of beasts (behema), and of fowl . . ." The wisest man of all time spoke of the real world of plants and animals he knew—including the real animals referred to as behema.

The next use is in context of the great drought caused famine that was called into existence by Elijah against the wicked King Ahab. Ahab ordered one of his servants to go out to try to find some water source that still supported grass " . . . to save the horses and mules alive, that we lose not all the beasts (behema)." The English word horse here is the Hebrew word cuwc and according to Strong's means "to skip". Other English words that this Hebrew word is transliterated into are 'swallow' and 'crane'. It would appear that horse is just a transliterated guess on the part of the translators; but the description given by God of a horse (cuwc) in Job 39 and of a horse's hoof in Ezekiel 26 really sounds more like a dragon than an English horse! My research notes are interspersed with the texts. Scripture is bolded, my notes in normal print. See for yourself:

"[Job 39 God speaking] **'Hast thou given the horse** (cuwc-5483) **strength** (1369-gebuwrah-fem of 1368-gibbowr!)**? Hast thou clothed his neck** (6677-tsavvar) **with thunder** (7483-ramah-quivering in the wind)**? Canst thou make him afraid as a grasshopper? The glory** (1935-howd-grandeur, imposing form) **of his nostrils** (5170-nacharahsnort {up to this point in OT a different word is used for nostrils; only in Job is 5170 and 5156 in Leviathan passage used}) **terrible! He paweth** (2658-chaphar-to pry into, dig) **in the valley and rejoiceth in his strength** (3581-kowach-vigor [of a large lizard!]); **he goeth on to meet the armed men! He mocketh at fear and is not affrighted; neither turneth he back from the sword; the quiver rattleth against him and the glittering spear and the shield. He swalloweth the ground with fierceness** (7494-raash-vibration, commotion[from 7493-to undulate, quake, tremble]—this word is also used to describe physical EARTHQUAKES!—could a modern horse evoke such comparisons?) **and rage** (7267-rogez-commotion, restlessness, crash [of thunder]); **neither believeth he the sound of the trumpet** (7782-showphar)! **He saith among the trumpets, "Ha, ha!" and he smelleth** (7306-ruwach-to blow, breathe, anticipate) **the battle afar off; the thunder of the captains and the shouting!"'**–and Ezekiel 26 again God speaking, **'With the hoofs** (6541-parcah-claw or cloven footed {NOTE: Horse's hooves are NOT divided! If the claw of a dragon or raptor; matches nicely with Job}) **of his horses** (5483) . . . '

The Hebrew word for mules in the passage is 'pered'—derived from the root parad meaning "to disperse, divide or sunder". The English word 'mules' then is also a transliteration. We do not really know what animals are identified except that they are behema and so they are logically a type of dinosaur—and that the king desires to save his most precious animals if possible. This would mean he wanted to save his pet dinosaurs, not other more easily obtained or replaced creatures.

Were behema also used in battle? Check out the reference found at 2 Kings 3:9 and 3:17. The successor to the northern kingdom of Israel's King Ahab is Jehoram—who went out to put down a revolt staged by the Moabites. He asked King Jehosaphat of southern kingdom of Judah to go into battle with him. King Jehosaphat agreed and their combined armies marched south into a dry part of Israel near the south end of the modern day Dead Sea. Apparently they were expecting to find sufficient water for an army but did not and were in a little bit of a jam as " . . . there was no water for the host, and for the cattle (behemoth) that followed them."

Fortunately Elisha the prophet lived nearby and King Jehosaphat was on good terms with him. The King of Judah asked the prophet to enquire of God to see what He might be willing to do. Elisha did so and brought God's answer in verses 16-18, "Make this valley full of ditches . . . . You shall not see wind, neither shall you see rain, yet that valley shall be filled with water, that you may drink, both you, and your cattle (miqneh-acquired livestock), and your beasts (behema)." The behema were either there to be a platform from which to fight, like the 'olephants' in the recent hit movie <u>The Lord of the Rings: The Return of the King</u>, or as a food source—or both! One good sized brachiosaurus would feed an army for a while!

There are five occurrences of behema / behemoth in the books of 1 and 2 Chronicles. The first appears at 1 Chronicles 5:21 where again behemoth were taken as a prize of victory in battle. In 1 Chronicles 7:21 there was an unsuccessful raid on an enemy to steal away his behemoth. Another battle where behemoth was one object of spoil is found in 2 Chronicles 14:15. In 2 Chronicles 26:10 the king of Judah named Uzziah " . . . dug many wells, for he had much cattle (behemoth), both in the low country and in the plains . . ." The final use of behema is 2 Chronicles 32:28 where King Hezekiah has built "Storehouses also for the increase of corn, and wine, and oil; and stalls for all manner of beasts (behema) . . . ." King Hezekiah built cages for his pet behema! Obviously there were many different kinds of behema!

Nehemiah is the first book where every use of the word cattle is behemoth and every use of the word beast is the word behema! Do you want to see a man riding a dinosaur? Turn to Nehemiah 2:1-4. Nehemiah has just returned to the destroyed city of Jerusalem from serving as cupbearer to the king of Persia—to survey the situation and rebuild the wall. He hasn't told anyone of his mission and decides to take a look at the city by moonlight. He chooses his trusty mount and takes off. Half way around the city he runs into a problem; the beast (behema) upon which he was riding could not fit through the ruined city gate! Yes! Nehemiah records that he was riding on a behema!—not a 'horse' (cuwc) or 'ox/cow' (baqar or showr). He could have chosen those words if that is what he meant. Nehemiah chose the word behema because that is what he was riding on!

Remember: Nehemiah had just come from Persia. The Persians and Medes had recently conquered the Babylonian empire. The wall of the city of Babylon bears the images of dragons. About 1500 years later; Marco Polo records in his journals that the kings of the east used dragons to pull their carts. Why wouldn't an official of an eastern king on an official mission for that king use some of the royal dragons? Of course; if that official were a captive Hebrew—that official would record the events in his native tongue and use the equivalent word for dragon: Behema.

I have been to the city of Jerusalem. I have walked through the gates that would have been burned and broken down by the Babyonians when they conquered Judah. The gates are at least 15 feet wide. The point is: An elephant with a rider would have no problem getting through width-wise; as elephants are not that wide. An adult Brachiosaurus would be a different matter. An animal the size of 10 school busses and up to 100 feet long would find it very difficult to get through a 15 foot wide gate.

Ezra was a contemporary of Nehemiah and also exclusively uses behema for the two times the English word 'beasts' is used. The first is at Ezra 1:4 where the order from king Cyrus goes out for the Jews who are not willing to return to Jerusalem to help those who are with " . . . silver, and with gold, and with goods, and with beasts (behema) . . .". The behema apparently are going to pull the wagons or be ridden or both. Ezra 1:6 says the people did supply all the things required. The silver and gold were real, so were the behema. The King of Persia would not be telling the people to provide a mythical creature—but would order those not willing to make the sacrifice of going to Jerusalem to resettle the city to make a major sacrifice in other ways: Gold, silver, behema—their most valuable items.

The book of Job where all this talk began with the mention of a behemoth—uses the word behema three times. The first is found at Job 12:7 where Job is making answer to one of his accusers, um—I mean, friends, "But ask now the beasts (behema), and they shall teach you . . ." Is it not cool that God takes Job's own advice and uses a type of behema called a behemoth to make His timeless point? Could it be further proof of the grouping term nature of the word behema?—for when God speaks from chapter 39 to 41; He mentions the cuwc (probably a dragon), the behemoth (brachiosaurus) and Leviathan (greatest of sea monsters).

In Job 18:3 Bildad the Shuhite says, "Wherefore are we counted as beasts (behema)?" The final advisor of Job is Elihu who speaks to Job in chapter 35:11 "Who teaches us more than the beasts (behema) of the earth . . . ." It would seem that these persons; all apparently real—are quite familiar with the animals known as behema and behemoth. In our day and age; satan has corrupted our understanding of dinosaurs and is teaching us his lying doctrine of millions of years and man without dinosaurs **in our public schools** *at taxpayer expense!* Both God and satan know that these creatures command the attention of man in a way little else does.

The concepts taught in public schools today are the lying doctrines of the religion of evolution. Why is the taxpayer's money—confiscated by government via a Marxist income tax—being used to teach a religious view when these same people say tenets of the Christian religion cannot be taught there? If one religious view can be taught at public expense—why cannot others? Some weakly claim that 'evolution is science!' and creation concepts are religion. This is another lie of satan!

For any concept to be science it must have two traits: 1) It must be observable in the present time {neither evolution nor creation can be observed presently taking place} 2) It must be repeatable so that others can verify or falsify it (again; neither evolution nor creation can be repeated). Both creation and evolution are religious constructs of unobserved history! Neither view is science—and so **neither should be taught in Science class in public school.** However; if one is being taught (evolution is)—the other should also be taught to be fair. Any third, fourth or more possibilities (I know of none and I have studied this issue for at least ten years) should also be taught. **Taxpayers of America—you are being ripped off! Christians of America— your money is being used to further the enemy's kingdom!** The only way to fix this sad situation is to elect school board candidates that will pay for both to be taught or remove evolution from Science class!

In the Psalms; 11 occurrences of behema are found. The first is in chapter 8 at verse 7 and is a very well known psalm of David, "O Lord!

Our Lord! How excellent is Thy Name in all the earth! . . . . When I consider Thy heavens, the work of Thy fingers . . . . what is man, that Thou art mindful of him? . . . . Thou madest him to have dominion over the works of Thy hands . . . . All sheep and oxen, yea, and the beasts (behema) of the field . . . ." King David; musing over all the wonders of God; includes behema in the list!

The next time behema is used is another Psalm authored by King David. Psalm 36:6 affirms yet again the special place these creatures have in God's providence, " . . . O Lord, Thou preservest man and beast (behema)." In Psalm 49 behema appears twice; both in reference to man and beast perishing because they are mortal.

Unbelievably, the next occurrence is found in one of the most recognizable verses from the Psalms. Psalm 50:10 says, "For every beast (chay) of the forest is Mine, and the cattle (behemoth) upon a thousand hills." There must have been very many behemoth indeed!—and they lived on hills, not just in the swamps. The verse that so many quote to describe the riches of God includes the incredible animals known as behemoth.

Yet another huge surprise awaits in the next reference found in Psalm 73:22 "So foolish was I, and ignorant: I was as a beast (behema) before thee." Asaph (or another unknown person) is pouring out his heart to God; trying to understand why wicked people prosper in this life—as they still do in our day. Then Asaph enters the sanctuary of God and sees that the wicked will ultimately and eternally perish; separated from God forever. He proclaims that he has been as a dumb animal in his worry and anxiety. He expects God will recognize the real animal he names.

Psalm 104, 107, 147 and 148 exclaim the goodness of God in providing for all He has made and does not fail to include the behema / behemoth. Psalm 135:8 recalls the plague of death on the first born of Egypt and affirms that the plague was on " . . . the firstborn of Egypt, both man and beast (behema)." In 104:14, "He causeth the grass to grow for the cattle (behemoth), . . .", 107:38, " . . . and suffereth not their cattle (behemoth) to decrease.", 147:9, "He giveth grass to the beast (behema) . . ." and 148:10, "Beasts (chay), and all cattle (behemoth) . . .". Many Bible scholars believe Psalms 145-150 were written by Hezekiah—the king that had built many pens for his pet dinosaurs does not fail to mention his prize pets in his psalms! Notice the comfortableness with which the writers across the centuries refer to real animals that must be dinosaurs.

Proverbs uses behema for one out of two times beast appears in English. The single reference is found in chapter 12 at verse 10, "The righteous man regardeth the life of his beast (behema), but the tender mercies of the wicked are cruel." Solomon uses behema in one of his recorded 3000 proverbs as a real and valuable animal; just as was claimed in the book of Kings. Solomon then proceeds to use behema every time beast or beasts is mentioned in Ecclesiastes. All four uses occur in chapter 3 from verses 18-21 and Solomon compares the lot of men as the same as for beasts (behema) with the possible exception of where their spirits go upon death "Who knoweth the spirit of man that goeth upward and the spirit of the beast (behema) that goeth downward . . .". So impressive an animal is the behema / behemoth that the great Solomon wonders if its spirit will go to heaven!

Summary of main points:

1) Behema and behemoth were very valuable animals—often taken as war spoils
2) Many writers over more than a thousand years consistently use behema and behemoth
3) King David and king Solomon wrote of these creatures as if they were real animals—not some kind of mythical creature
4) God takes special note of these great creatures, often tying their welfare and fate to man's

CHAPTER SIX

The Prophets Speak of
Behema / Behemoth

The greatest prophet of Israel's history without doubt is Isaiah. The prophet to the great king Hezekiah and the one who prophesied so clearly about the Coming, Nature, and Mission of the Messiah—used the word behema or behemoth five times in his writings. The first two uses occurs in chapter 18 at verse 6 where the prophet is predicting the fall of Ethiopia; the fallen shall become food for " . . . the beasts (behema) of the earth: and the fowls shall summer upon them, and all the beasts (behema) of the earth shall winter upon them." The next reference is found in chapter 30 verse 6 where the prophet warns that the children of Israel will not be saved by depending on and allying with Egypt.

In the same passage another wonderful animal is introduced, "The burden of the beasts (behema) of the south . . . . from whence come the young and old lion (roarer); the viper; and fiery flying serpent (seraph-burning) . . ." A flying reptile? Where have we heard of these before? If Isaiah speaks of the behema as a real animal that people are very familiar with; he is also describing a real animal here. Next is a reference to domesticated behemoth bearing burdens in chapter 46:1 " . . . their idols were upon the beasts (chay), and upon the cattle (behemoth) . . ."

There are simply too many references over too long a period of time by too many reputable writers for behema / behemoth to be some kind of mythical creature! In our day; it has been pointed out that even in Chinese restaurants where the placemat depicts the twelve critters of the Chinese zodiac: All are real creatures still alive today; except possibly one; which also happens to be the greatest of all the critters: The dragon! Why all real animals—and then one mythical one? Would it not make more sense that all were real animals at the time the Chinese zodiac was created? It may be that the dragon has gone extinct or nearly extinct—but would it not make more sense to conclude all the animals were real and familiar at the inception of the Chinese zodiac?

The final time Isaiah uses behema is in chapter 63:14 to describe how the Lord came to the rescue of Israel after punishing them for rebelling against Him, "As a beast (behema) goeth down into the valley . . . ." If the behema is coming down into the valley, some types of behema must at least some of the time venture into the hills, as at the city of Ai back in Joshua and in Psalm 50. All of the references back each other up. A very clear interpretation is taking shape; perhaps because: It is the *correct* interpretation.

Jeremiah uses the word behema 19 of 26 times when the English is rendered beast / beasts. The first is found in chapter 7 at verses 20 and again in verse 33, "{20} . . . thus saith the Lord ' . . . Mine anger . . . shall be poured out upon . . . . man, and upon beast (behema) . . . {33} And the carcases of this people shall be meat for the fowls of the heaven, and for the beasts (behema) of the earth . . . ' The people of Israel had finally become so corrupt that God was going to treat them just like He treated the heathen nations He had destroyed to establish His people in the Promised Land.

Jeremiah—quoted from at length and revered by both Jew and Christian—uses the word behema many more times. Chapter 9 verse 10 contains the following, "For the mountains will I take up a weeping . . . . because they are burned up . . . neither can men hear the voice of the cattle (miqneh), both the fowl of the heavens and the beast (behema) are fled . . ." Again, we hear of behema living on hills and even low mountains. More references are found in chapter 12 at verse 4, " . . . the beasts (behema) are consumed . . ."

More warnings of impending doom come from God regarding His terrible judgment in Jeremiah 15:3, 16:4 and 19:7, "{15:3} And I will appoint over them . . . the sword to slay, and the dogs to tear, and the fowls of the heaven, and the beasts (behema) of the earth, to devour and destroy . . . . {16:4} . . . and their carcasses shall be meat for the fowls of heaven, and for the beasts (behema) of the earth . . . . {19:7} . . . and their carcasses will I give to be meat for the fowls of the heaven, and for the beasts (behema) of the earth." Swords, dogs, fowls are real things or creatures—so are behema.

The promised judgment will fall on Jerusalem, says God in Jeremiah 21:6, "And I will smite the inhabitants of this city, both man and beast (behema) . . ." God's total destruction judgment last fell on Jericho and most of the tribe of Benjamin. This punishment will now be delivered by the Babyonian King Nebuchadnezzar as foretold in chapter 27:6, "And now have I given all these lands into the hand of Nebuchadnezzar . . . and the beasts (behema) of the field have I given him . . . ." The Lord God, the Creator, gives the best of all lands into the hands of this pagan king, chosen to punish His sinning people (America—do not think He will let us go unpunished for our national sins!). The behema will become his as well, another prized spoil of conquest. After the fall of Babylon and end of the Jewish exile; Nehemiah would take some of the royal behema captured and used by the Persian king on his mission back to Jerusalem. Again, one section of Scripture backs up another.

Jeremiah 31-33 contains several references to behema. These are the passages where God promises to spend His wrath and then restore Israel, "{31:27} 'Behold, the days come . . . ' saith the Lord, 'that I will sow the house of Israel and the house of Judah with the seed of man, and with the seed of beast (behema) . . . . {32:43} And fields shall be bought in this land, whereof ye say, it is desolate without man or beast (behema). {33:10} . . . Again there shall be heard in this place, which ye say . . . without man and without beast (behema) . . . and in the streets of Jerusalem, that are desolate, without man . . . and without beast (behema)" Behema are apparently known on the very streets of Jerusalem!

Sometimes a prophecy is fulfilled quickly. The prophecy given just a few months or years before regarding the conquest of Nebuchadnezzar had come to the gates of Jerusalem. Jeremiah now addresses a more urgent and final warning to the rebellious king of Judah named Zedekiah, "{34:20} I will give them into the hand of their enemies . . . and their dead bodies shall be for meat unto the fowls of the heaven, and to the beasts (behema) of the earth."

Jeremiah's prophecies are not written in chronological order. A prophetic word given to an earlier king named Jehoiakim had been burned in contempt. As a result, Jeremiah sent another warning, "{36:29} And thou shalt say to Jehoiakim king of Judah, thus saith the Lord; thou hast burned this roll, saying, Why hast thou written . . . the king of Babylon shall . . . cause to cease from thence man and beast (behema)?"

One day the pagan empire of Babylon will be punished for her sins and Jeremiah predicts this event more than 60 years in the future, "{50:3} For out of the north there cometh up a nation against her . . . they shall remove . . . . both man and beast (behema). {51:62} . . . that none shall remain in it, neither man nor beast (behema) . . . ." These critters will be taken into the capital city of Persia, from where Nehemiah will take some when he goes to rebuild Jerusalem.

The prophet Ezekiel also uses behema frequently. Of the 25 references to beast or beasts, 13 are behema. The first occurs in chapter 8 at verse 10 where Ezekiel is experiencing a vision of God. He is transported to Jerusalem and is shown the idolatry the ancients were condoning in the Temple courts, "So I went in and saw, and behold!—every form of creeping things—and abominable (filthy-unclean) beasts (behema) . . . portrayed upon the wall . . ." This passage further underscores the idea that Solomon's making of graven oxen (baqar) was not punishable, but these people violated the command against making graven images of the unclean behema—the connotation is that they intended to or were worshipping these greatest creatures rather than the Creator. If that Temple had not been destroyed; we might have been able to recover those images as we have recovered the images of dragons on the walls of Babylon.

Next comes a series of uses in a single chapter. The exiled elders of Israel come to Ezekiel and God tells him of the idolatry in their hearts. The judgment will be fully executed upon them, "{14:13} . . . I will break the staff of bread thereof, and will send famine upon it, and will cut off man and beast (behema) from it." The punishment is so sure to happen that God says that even if Noah, Daniel, and Job were in Jerusalem, only they would be saved, upon the rest, "{14:17} . . . I bring a sword upon the land . . . I cut off man and beast (behema) . . . .

{14:19} . . . I send a pestilence into the land . . . to cut off man and beast (behema) . . . {14:21} . . . I send My sore judgments upon Jerusalem, the sword, the famine, and the noisome beast (behema) and the pestilence to cut off from it man and beast (behema)." God is using the word behema just as He has in numerous situations over the last several thousand years of Biblical history. Noah, Daniel and Job were real persons; why would behema not be real animals? They were real!—and very important: Economically—Militarily—Symbolically.

Then a quick series of prophecies against Edom, an ancient enemy of Israel, and Egypt confirms that these civilizations, too, were familiar with behema, "{25:13} . . . I will also stretch out Mine hand upon Edom, and will cut off man and beast (behema) from it . . . {29:8&11} Behold I will bring a sword upon thee, and cut off man and beast (behema) . . . No foot of man shall pass through it, nor foot of beast (behema) . . . . forty years. {32:13} I will destroy also all the beasts (behema) thereof from beside the great waters; neither shall the foot of man trouble them any more nor the hoofs of beasts (behema) trouble them."

Then, like Isaiah and Jeremiah before him, Ezekiel is shown what God will do after His anger is spent, "{36:11} And I will multiply upon you man and beast (behema) . . . better unto you than at your beginnings . . ." God obviously loves the creatures He made called behema for they are specifically mentioned again!

The final occurrence of behema in Ezekiel is in chapter 44:31, "The priests shall not eat of any thing that is dead of itself, or torn, whether it be fowl or beast (behema)." Finally, no more having to guess, behema were considered a food source! Brontoburgers anyone?

Curiously the book of Daniel has no uses of behema. One would think that his being captive in Babylon where dragons seem to have been worshipped as well as pressed into service; at least one reference would be present. There are many references to beasts as the Chaldean equivalent to the Hebrew word for chay—living thing and so this may be yet another word that encompasses or means dinosaur.

All three times beast or beasts is used by the prophet Joel—it is the word behema. Chapter 1:18 reads, "How do the beasts (behema) groan!

The herds of cattle (baqar-beeves) are perplexed . . ." This passage again shows that oxen / cows are not behema. Next comes 1:20, "The beasts (behema) of the field cry also unto Thee . . ." Finally, chapter 2 verse 22 tells us what at least some of the behema eat besides grass, "Be not afraid, ye beasts (behema) of the field: for the pastures . . . . do spring, for the tree beareth her fruit, the fig tree and the vine do yield their strength." So these creatures; some of which sometimes feed on carrion of battle slain—also eat other vegetation beside grass. Some researchers believe even the mighty T-rex was primarily a plant eater. They point out the shallow root structure of those great, six-inch long teeth—saying they are better suited to stripping leaves off of trees than tearing meat from bodies.

Jonah also exclusively uses the word behema / behemoth to describe cattle and beasts. The words appear 3 times in four chapters. In chapter 3, after Jonah wisely decided to obey God and gave the message to the Ninivites: The king of Nineveh ordered an unusual fast. Not only were people to forego food, but so were the behema, "{3:7} . . . Let neither man nor beast (behema) . . . taste any thing: let them not feed, nor drink water." The king also ordered another unusual demonstration of repentance, "{3:8} But let man and beast (behema) be covered with sackcloth and cry mightily unto God . . ." It is one thing for men to fast and humble themselves; but for man to humble his greatest animals, too! Perhaps this extra show of contrition on the part of the Ninevites is the reason God forgave their great wickedness. The last use reasserts the close connection between behemoth and behema, "{4:11} Should I not spare Nineveh . . . wherein are more than six-score thousand persons . . . and also much cattle (behemoth)?" Can any doubt remain that behema either are or include behemoth?

The next occurrence of behema is astounding! The prophet Micah, in the same passage as he predicts where the Savior will be born tells us, "{5:8} And the remnant of Jacob shall be among the Gentiles in the midst of many people—as a lion (roarer) among the beasts (behema) of Israel . . ." Is the lion also a type of dinosaur? The word only means that the critter roars—lions roar today, but in all the movies—the raptor dinosaurs roar also. There are many different types of 'lions' in the Old Testament as well.

Not only is the word behema used frequently but is also used in some prominent places! Habakkuk continues the use of behema in prominent passages such as where the doctrine of salvation by faith is articulated in 2:4 the passage continues to the end of the chapter including, "{2:17} For the violence of Lebanon shall cover thee, and the spoil of beasts (behema), which made them afraid . . ."

The opening prophecy of Zephaniah 1:1-18 includes yet another example of God identifying behema as a very special creature, closely associated with man, "{1:3} I will consume man and beast (behema) . . ." The prophecy of Zechariah clearly tells us that behema were domesticated animals, "{8:10} For before these days there was no hire for man, nor any hire for beast (behema) . . . ."

The final use of behema in the Old Testament is also found in Zechariah, in the description of the final battle against God by His enemies. The scene is very frightening as some kind of incredible plague will come upon the enemies of God including all their animals, "{14:15} And so shall be the plague of the horse, of the mule, of the camel, and of the ass, and of all the beasts (behema) that shall be in these tents . . ." Behema may not be horses, mules, camels or asses—or all are types of behema; I am not that much of a Hebrew scholar to know. They are distinct animals that play incredibly important—if currently little understood—roles in the life of the Hebrew people.

Approximately four thousand years have passed—from beginning to end filled with references to animals we in our day call dinosaurs. The most reputable writers in all the history of mankind: Moses, Isaiah, Jeremiah, Ezekiel, King David, King Solomon—not to mention the majority of the time it is God Himself—all use behema, behemoth, tanniyn, owph, cuwc, chamowr and many other names for creatures that were dinosaurs. Some of those fanciful movies showing men riding dragons or brachiosaurs, etc—are showing us things that actually happened—though the makers of these movies do not believe it to be anything but legend themselves.

Summary of main points:

1) Behema and behemoth are clearly real creatures, used for food and labor and possibly as fighting platforms, involved heavily or exclusively in Jewish worship

2) There are still questions to be answered due to the author's lack of ability in the Hebrew language, but there is certainly enough smoke to indicate there is a fire somewhere—man and dinosaur have always lived together

3) The evolution religion is completely wrong—since men and dinosaurs lived together and interacted in many ways

Moses' Staff

If you saw the epic movie, <u>The Ten Commandments</u>, who can forget the dramatic showdown between Moses (Charlton Heston) and Pharaoh's magicians! Staves turn into snakes and Moses' snake proceeds to gobble up the magician's snakes and all are impressed! Is that what really happened? Again; let us consult the Hebrew words that record the account.

Once I realized that some Hebrew words can be translated / transliterated into different English words and that different Hebrew words are often translated /transliterated into the same English word: I decided to look up EVERY animal and animal part or feature or characteristic mentioned in the Bible in my Strong's. A short time later; God put it on my heart to retype the entire Bible so that I would be forced to encounter every animal and body part of an animal and every contextual use of an animal—and record this information for whoever may make use of it.

The Bible retype effort took a while, as ancient society was much more agricultural based than American society is today. There are a lot of animals mentioned! That work is called <u>The King James II Bible: Only The Words of God!—with Glenn's notations</u>. For the time being, it is available to anyone who will cover the $5 production and mailing cost and tell me why they need it. Every animal or part or use of animal has the word from Strong's beside it and my commentary with it. There are also some other commentaries made in it on other points of interest.

Since I was interested in dinosaurs in particular and found the real uses of behemoth / behema by God's sovereign grace—I looked up the Hebrew word that had been rendered into English as dragon. The

Hebrew word for dragon is tanniyn (#8577 in Strong's). Tanniyn means "monster" and is translated into the three English words; dragon(s), whale(s) and serpent(s) in the King James Bible. Some other versions of Dr. Strong's work claim that the word should also stand for jackal(s), but the KJB never translates that word that way.

Remember; the KJB was created in 1611 while the world's vastly prevailing belief was that the Bible was true and the earth was only thousands of years old. All of the other translations were made when evolution was gaining popularity and so some alternative understanding for man with dinosaurs would be necessary to pull off the deception of 'billions of years' and 'no men with dinosaurs' scam. If you wonder what the mindset of men in America was as little as 200 years ago; get a copy of Knickerbocker's <u>A History of New York</u>. The author opens his book with a derisive chastisement of all the fables of mankind regarding the origin of the world. In the end, he endorses the 'account left to us by Moses . . . ' as the Truth. This book was the greatest bestseller of that day, obviously the people of that period believed the Bible was historically true. How different our world would be today if we still believed this.

The persons who did not have their minds filled with 'millions of years' dogma never used the word jackal to transliterate the Hebrew word tanniyn; but those whose minds have been exposed to evolution ideas did {the new versions of Strong's}! The root Hebrew word for tanniyn is tan; meaning 'to elongate or monster'. A jackal is a medium sized dog. To claim that tanniyn is a dog does unspeakable violence to the original meaning! The word tanniyn is used 27 times in the Old Testament. Two other times another word meaning essentially the same thing is used; tannah and tan (the root word itself, by itself).

If the tanniyn lives in the water, it is a monster in the sea—a sea monster. The first occurrence of the Hebrew word tanniyn (monster) is in Genesis 1:21 on the fifth day of creation—the day God made the sea creatures (more than just the fish) and the fowls (not just birds, but we will get to that later). In verse 21, after mentioning fish, plankton / krill and winged creatures; God specifically tells us of His final created sea creature, "And God created great whales (tanniyn)." Since these monsters live in the sea; the verse more accurately may be rendered

"And God created great sea monsters." At least one modern translation does render the word and phrase literally.

Sea monsters may indeed include the huge whales; but would also include other large monsters of the sea such as Plesiosaurs, Zooglodons, etc. All manner of large, air breathing (non-fish, non-plankton) life in the sea could be included—or it could also be that ONLY marine dragons are in mind. One particular type of sea monster is the famous Leviathan of Job chapter 41. Apparently this sea dragon writhed and had the ability to breathe fire and smoke. Here is the passage from Job 41 with my notes included; again Scripture in bold:

'**Canst thou draw out leviathan** (3882-livyathan-wreathed serpent) **with an hook; or his tongue with a cord thou lettest down? Canst thou put an hook into his nose or bore his jaw through with a thorn? Will he make many supplications unto thee; will he speak soft unto thee? Will he make a covenant with thee; wilt thou take him for a servant for ever? Wilt thou play with him as a bird or wilt thou bind him for thy maidens? Shall the companions make a banquet of him** (apparently men hunted sea monsters for food or to boil out oil—reference the 1800s ship Monongahela killing a sea monster and processing its fat into oil for fuel)**? Shall they part him among the merchants? Canst thou fill his skin with barbed irons or his head with fish spears?**

'**Lay thine hand upon him; remember the battle and do no more! Behold; the hope of him is in vain!—shall not be cast down?—even at the sight of him! None fierce** (393-akzar-brave) **that dare stir him up!—who then is able to stand before Me? Who hath prevented Me that I should repay? Under the whole heaven: Is Mine! I will not conceal** (2790-charash-to scratch, to engrave, to fabricate) **his parts** (905-bad-separation, part of body, [like] a branch of a tree) **nor his power; nor his comely proportion** (6187-erek-equipment-[from 6186-arak-to set in a row]).

'**Who can discover** (1540-galah-to denude) **the face** (6440-paniym) **of his garment? Who can come with his double bridle** (7448-recen-to curb, a halter as restraining the jaw)**? Who can open the doors** (1817-deleth-something swinging, two leaved gate or leaf or lid NOTE: Could this be large projections from each side of the face of a dragon? Many depictions of dragons sport this feature) **of his face** (6440)**? His teeth** (8127-shen-tooth, ivory) **terrible round about; scales** (650,4043-aphiyq {containing a tube; used for behemoth to describe his bones}meginnah-a small shield NOTE: Different word than used in Leviticus to describe things from the waters that may be eaten; fins and scales; apparently these scales are boney and very strong) **pride** (1346-gaavah-majestic)**!—shut up together!—a close seal!—one is so near to another that no air can come between them. They are joined** (1692-dabaq-cleave) **one to another!—they stick** (3920-lakad-cohere) **together that they cannot be sundered** (6504-parad-separate, break through, be out of joint).

'**By his neesings** (5846-atiyshah-sneeze/ing) **a light** (216-owr-lightning[from 215-owr-luminous, set on fire]) **doth shine** (1984-halal-be clear, make a show) **and his eyes like the eyelids of the morning** (7837-shachar). **Out of his mouth go burning-lamps** (3940-lappiyd-flame, lightning)**; sparks** (3590-kiydowd-struck off) **of fire leap** (4422-malat-be smooth, escape) **out. Out of his nostrils goeth smoke as of a seething pot or caldron. His breath** (5315-nephesh) **kindleth** (3857-lahat-to lick, blaze) **coals** (1513-gechel-glow, ember) **and a flame** (3851-lahab-gleam, flash) **goeth out of his mouth. In his neck remaineth strength and sorrow is turned into joy** (8643-teruwah-clamor, a battle-cry, alarm, loud noise) **before him. The flakes** (4651-mappal-falling off, chaff; pendulous, a flap—NOTE: wings; scales or flippers?) **of his flesh** (1320-basar-body) **are joined together; they are firm** (3332-yatsaq-to pour out, cast as metal) **in themselves; they cannot be moved. His heart** (3820-leb-the heart {when describing an organ}; will or courage or any of a wide number of other feelings) **is as firm as a stone; yea, as hard as a piece of the nether** (8482-tachtiy-lowermost part).

'**When he raiseth up himself, the mighty** (410-el-strong{short form of 352-ayil}) **are afraid by reason of breakings** (7667-sheber-destruction) **they purify** (2398-chata-to miss, to forfeit, purge) **themselves.** [NOTE: Seems God is saying 'they pee their pants for fear or are even scared to literal death']. **The sword of him that layeth at him cannot hold; the spear, the dart nor the habergeon. He esteemeth iron as straw; brass as rotten wood. The arrow**

cannot make him flee; slingstones are turned with him into stubble. Darts are counted as stubble; he laugheth at the shaking of a spear. Sharp stones (2789-cheres-pot sherd) **under him; he spreadeth** (7502-raphad-make a bed) **sharp-pointed things upon the mire** (2916-tiyt-be sticky, mud or clay)**. He maketh the deep to boil like a pot. He maketh the sea like a pot of ointment. He maketh a path** (5410-nathiyb-to tramp, track) **to shine** (215-owr-luminous) **after him; would think the deep hoary. Upon the earth there is not his like who is made without fear. He beholdeth all high. He!—a king over all the children of pride.'**

This is the same God describing Leviathan as described Behemoth one chapter earlier. God apparently believes that He created fire breathing sea monsters with which men of Job's day are very familiar!

Is fire breathing possible? This is God speaking here! If you doubt the characteristics; you doubt God's account! Still—for the Thomas's in the audience—an example of fire squirting from the abdomen of an insect can be observed in nature today. The Bombardier beetle can propel chemicals from its body that undergo a combustion reaction in the presence of oxygen in the atmosphere—essentially shooting fire—if a bug can do it; why not a dragon? The temptation may be to disbelieve what we have not witnessed ourselves—but more than 75% of life's 'facts' are taken on faith in a written or oral statement that we choose to believe. Something as basic as your own name is nothing more than a few words on a piece of paper. You could have been switched in the hospital for all you know! I prefer to believe God until He is proved incorrect (since this has never happened)—rather than believe men (who are proved wrong continually on all sorts of issues). You may make your own choice.

Did Noah take tanniyn on the ark with him? If they were to survive the Flood; at least the land tanniyn would have to go. The sea monsters would be just fine and some of them may have become trapped in large inland lakes when the Flood waters drained away. Can you say 'Nessie'? I thought you could; if you tried. Suddenly all the accounts of large marine reptiles do not sound so crazy! Tanniyn are not mentioned specifically as having entered the ark. That is not fatal to my premise; many subdivisions of animals are not specifically mentioned as going on the Ark during Noah's Flood; but appear later: The implication being that they must have been on the Ark. The land dwelling tanniyn apparently were a subdivision of a much larger group known as 'beasts of the earth / field'. Another possibility is that the tanniyn are the unclean beasts (behema) because technically; even a T-rex is a quadruped with four legs.

Genesis 1:24 says "And God said, 'Let the earth bring forth the living creature after his kind; cattle, creeping things and the beasts of the earth." Cattle, as previously noted; is behemoth, creeping things are defined as the little skittery critters and beasts of the earth apparently cover everything between large quadrupeds and mice, i.e. sheep, cows, deer, Komodo Dragons and such. Beasts of the earth / field must logically include medium sized reptiles with four legs because of the passage in Genesis 3, "Now the serpent was more subtle than all the other beasts of the field . . . ." The serpent known as nachash at that moment still had his legs because God did not curse them off until verse 14, " . . . upon your belly shall you go . . ." The Hebrew word for serpent {nachash} after the loss of legs is the same as before the event. So medium sized; four-legged reptiles were a subdivision of the grouping of animals known as "beasts of the earth / field". Again I appeal to the Hebrew scholars to sort this all out better than I have been able to.

Beasts of the earth / field are mentioned as being passengers on the Ark. Beasts (behema) of the earth / field are also identified most frequently as being the critters that would feast on the war dead along with the fowls of the air. The next time we encounter a tanniyn in the Bible is on land and well after the Flood; still more evidence that tanniyn must be a subdivision of animal that entered the Ark either as unclean behema or beasts of the earth / field or both. This encounter is with none other than Moses; the writer of the book of Exodus in which it is found.

Moses has been driven from Egypt and found refuge herding sheep / goats for his father in law, Jethro of Midian. The location is the base of Mount Sinai. One day Moses sees a bush that burns with fire—yet is not consumed! Moses investigates and encounters God. During the discourse; Moses is told by God to throw his staff on the ground. We are informed that it becomes a serpent {English}. Later, before Pharaoh,

Moses tells Aaron to throw his staff on the ground to impress the pagan king. The staff turns into a serpent {English}. Pharaoh is not impressed and calls for his magicians who turn their staves into serpents {English}. This scene is portrayed in Cecil B. DeMille's <u>The Ten Commandments</u> as a snake fight—as would be expected from the English rendering.

Now let us look at this passage in the language that it was written in. At the burning bush, Moses' staff turns into nachash!—the hissing one that deceived the woman, later named Eve by Adam. Moses is told to take nachash by the tail—for it is Jesus who will bruise nachash's head. However, when Moses and Aaron are before Pharaoh; it is Aaron's staff that turns into tanniyn: A monster! Then Pharaoh's magician's staves turn into tanniyn—monsters! Then Aaron's monster eats up the Egyptian magician's monsters! Perhaps the scene from <u>Jurassic Park</u> in the laboratory where the T-rex eats up the two raptors should be in our mind. If Moses had meant that the staves before Pharaoh turned into nachash; snakes as popularly depicted—he could have used the word he chose to describe what happened at the burning bush a few sentences earlier. Moses chose tanniyn because that is what happened!

The actual words are in Exodus 7:9-12, "{7:9} When Pharaoh shall speak unto you; saying, 'Shew a miracle for you!'—then you shall say unto Aaron, 'Take thy rod and cast it before Pharaoh!'—and it shall become a serpent (tanniyn-monster)!' {7:10} And Moses and Aaron went in unto Pharaoh and they did so as the Lord had commanded—and Aaron cast down his rod before Pharaoh and before his servants—and it became a serpent (tanniyn). {7:11 &12} Then Pharaoh also called the wise men and the sorcerers. Now the magicians of Egypt; they also did in like manner with their enchantments—for they cast down every man his rod and they became serpents (tanniyn-monsters)—but Aaron's rod swallowed up their rods." This is a first hand eye-witness account rendered not by just any witness, but by Moses—the man we regard as the greatest Law-giver of all (via God of course)!

Moses uses the word tanniyn just one more time in his writings. Deuteronomy 32:33 reads, "Their wine is the poison of dragons (tanniyn) and the cruel venom of asps." We see that tanniyn are associated with poisonous bites, typical of reptiles and that they are not snakes (asps). This fact will take on more importance when we get to the Book of Acts.

Nehemiah; we now know—rode upon a behema during his tour of Jerusalem. One of the landmarks he notes riding by is, "{2:13} And I went out by night by the gate of the valley, even before the dragon (tanniyn-monster) well . . ." Apparently the gate of the valley was larger than the gate of the fountain that the behema he rode on could not pass through or his behema was located outside that gate.

Job, as we have already seen, contains the only reference to behemoth as the literal word behemoth. Job also contains a reference to tanniyn found in chapter 7 verse 12, "Am I a sea, or a whale (tan—sea monster), that Thou settest a watch over me?" Tan is the root word for tanniyn and means 'to elongate'. Notice how Job again affirms the special place in God's sight held by these great creatures.

The Psalms have 4 references to tanniyn. The first is found in Psalm 44:19, "Though thou hast sore broken us in the place of dragons (tanniyn) . . . . {44:20} If we have forgotten the name of our God, or stretched out our hands to a strange god . . ." David laments to God after an apparent defeat in battle.

Psalm 74:13 affirms that tanniyn may live in the water, "Thou didst divide the sea by Thy strength: Thou brakest the heads of the dragons (tanniyn) in the waters." The next verse tells us that Leviathan is in fact a specific kind of tanniyn, "{74:20} Thou brakest the heads of leviathan in pieces . . ." Did leviathan have more than one head? Again, perhaps some of the ancient legends were based on more reality that we thought!

Moving on to Psalm 91 at verse 13 we find in the great psalm of God's protection for those who put their trust in him that such persons will, " . . . tread upon the lion and the adder; the young lion and the dragon (tanniyn) shalt thou trample under feet." There is an interesting point here: The word lion is also transliterated. The basic word means "something that roars or a roarer". There may be no way to determine if this animal is actually the mammal we know today as a lion. For that matter; in the book of Samuel—David speaks to King Saul and claims to have fought both the lion and the bear: The word bear is transliterated and simply means "paw". Hebrew scholars, are you listening? Get off your glory-hallelujahs and figure some of this stuff out for us poor folks who wish we knew Hebrew better!

All creation praises God in its own way. The tanniyn are no exception as detailed in Psalm 148:7, "Praise the Lord from the earth ye dragons (tanniyn)—and from the deeps." This writer affirms that tanniyn live on land and in the ocean.

Isaiah was well acquainted with behema. He is no less familiar with dragons (tanniyn). Isaiah speaks of the future destruction of Babylon, before Babylon even becomes a world power! He tells us that, "{13:19-22} And Babylon . . . shall be as . . . Sodom and Gomorrah . . . It shall never be inhabited . . . but the wild beasts of the desert shall lie there . . . full of doleful creatures, and owls . . . and satyrs shall dance there . . . and dragons (tanniyn) in their pleasant palaces." Some say this has already happened with the defeat of Babylon by Medo-Persia. Some say this prophecy has yet to be fulfilled because in the middle of the prophecy we find that Babylon will, "never be inhabited". The city of Babylon was rebuilt by Saddam Hussein and is being used today. I find it very interesting that during Operation Iraqi Freedom; all cities were targeted as military targets except Babylon. In World War II; Rome was similarly avoided as a military target and is often referred to as the Great Babylon of Revelation. Hmmmm . . . .

Isaiah also identifies Leviathan as a sea monster in chapter 27:1, "In that day the Lord with His sore and great and strong sword shall punish Leviathan; the piercing serpent—even leviathan; that crooked serpent—and He shall slay the dragon (tanniyn) that is in the sea." Many have interpreted Leviathan to be Egypt in this prophecy; but why could it not be a real account of God showing man His power to conquer a creature so fierce that only God could do it?—especially after God has shown in Job that men could not hope to prevail against Leviathan.

Many of Isaiah's and Jeremiah's prophecies tell of severe judgment, Isaiah "{34:13} . . . it shall be an habitation of dragons (tanniyn) . . ." and Jeremiah 49:33 "And Hazor shall be a dwelling place for dragons (tanniyn)." Apparently some dragons are rather shy animals; but will move into the ruins of human civilization. Many trinket shops in popular tourist attractions have statues depicting dragons inhabiting ruined castles.

Chapter 35 of Isaiah tells of a time of restoring of the waste places and proclaims miracles of healing for people as well as, "{35:7} . . . the parched ground shall become a pool, and the thirsty land springs of water: in the habitation of dragons (tanniyn), where each lay, shall be grass with reeds and rushes." Notice again the wide range of habitats that dragons may inhabit; desert, wilderness, marshes, ruins of man's cities. Dragons seem to be quite versatile in their ability to adapt to environmental changes.

Another clue that tanniyn probably belong to that group of animals known as beasts of the earth is found in Isaiah 43:20, "The beast (chay-living thing) of the field shall honor me, the dragons (tanniyn) and the owls . . . ." The word 'owls' here is undefined in Strong's; so we have no idea what creature it actually is. Likewise, the final use of tanniyn in Isaiah is found in a verse that many have interpreted differently, "{51:9} . . . . Art thou not It that hath cut Rahab and wounded the dragon (tanniyn)?" Some say this is a figurative use of speech and that Rahab is the nation of Egypt. Other sections of prophecy in Isaiah deal with Egypt and call her by name. Could it be that Rahab is the name of another particularly fierce; land dwelling dragon that God alone could subdue like Leviathan?

Jeremiah uses tanniyn as many times as Isaiah. He also tells us that the ruins of Jerusalem will be, "{9:10&11} . . . the beast (behema) are fled . . . . And I will make Jerusalem heaps, and a den of dragons (tanniyn) . . . {10:22} . . . to make the cities of Judah desolate, and a den of dragons (tanniyn)." This prophecy agrees well with Nehemiah who passed by the dragon well {lair; den} when touring the ruins of Jerusalem some 70 years after Babylon conquered her! A literal interpretation is not out of the question!!

Jeremiah affirms that tanniyn had a great ability to detect smells from a long way off, "{14:6} . . . they snuffed up the wind like dragons (tanniyn)." Komodo dragons have been known to locate prey from more than a quarter of a mile by a keen sense of smell.

Jeremiah also foretells the fall of Babylon in even more detail than Isaiah and agrees with Isaiah both as to why Babylon will be punished and that it will be desolate. As for why punishment, it is because of the cruelty she executed on Israel, "{51:34} Nebuchadrezzar . . . hath devoured me, he hath crushed me . . . . he hath swallowed me up like a dragon (tanniyn)." But Babylon will become in her downfall, "And Babylon shall become heaps, a dwellingplace for dragons (tanniyn)." Komodo dragons and alligators tear large chunks of flesh from their prey and swallow it that way. The style of eating described here for dragons is consistent with what may be observed today of the closest animals we might or do call dragons.

Ezekiel uses tanniyn only once and it is clear from the context that it is to be considered a figurative use, "{29:3} Speak . . . I am against thee . . . Egypt, the great dragon (tanniyn) that lieth in the midst of his rivers, which hath said, My river . . . ." This passage must be viewed in a figurative light because the prophet links the metaphor to the subject.

The prophet Micah tells us of a sound that dragons can make, "{1:8} . . . I will wail and howl . . . like the dragons (tanniyn) . . . ." Apparently, dragons can remind a person of a human wailing in grief. Who knew so much information lay hidden in the pages we thought we knew so well.

The final Old Testament use of tanniyn occurs in the last book of the Old Testament; Malachi. This prophet agrees with the others that when God lays a land waste; it will become a desolate area only suitable for the "{1:3} . . . dragons (tannah) of the wilderness." This word is not tanniyn, but tannah—a female dragon; like the dragon from the movie <u>Shrek</u>.

The Old Testament has drawn to a close and four hundred years pass before the opening of the New Testament. In this time, great conquests described in the book of Daniel take place and the landscape is forever altered. It appears that behema and tanniyn fade into the distant memories for the land of Israel. It is possible that domesticating behema was a phenomena of the middle eastern cultures—though using behema to build massive structures could explain how the Acropolis was built. The Greeks may not have domesticated them; because there is an account of Alexander the Great's army being surprised and frightened by a behema. It appears these wonderful animals became more and more rare until chance encounters made the headlines. Marco Polo does record in his diaries that kings in the Far East used dragons to pull carts and the Ica Stones from Peru show dinosaurs and man interacting in a variety of ways.

A dictionary from the 1700's owned by Dr. Kent Hovind defines dragons as "now rare, but still living animals . . ." I have a dictionary from 1943 that defines dragons as "now rare . . ." If you look in most dictionaries from today, dragons are defined as, "mythical creatures . . ." Why has the definition changed? Not very many people have seen one and of those that have, even fewer are willing to admit that they saw either a dragon or a sea monster. Many that have do not wish to make the sighting known for fear that people will label them as lunatics.

It should not surprise us then that as encounters with these magnificent creatures occurred less and less frequently that the New Testament would have only a few general words for these creatures: Beast (therion) and dragon (drakon). In the New Testament; dragon is only found in Revelation as a figurative picture for satan. The English word beasts; which often is the Greek word therion; is used in many places and appears to be the Greek equivalent of the English dragon or carnivorous dinosaur. Serpents are referred to many times in the New Testament but are mostly the Greek word for snake or a figurative reference.

Summary of main points:

1) Dragons were real creatures
2) The creature that allowed satan to enter it was called Nachash and was a type of behemoth—possibly our modern creature called Anaconda
3) Dragons continued into New Testament times as the Greek word Therion—it is possible that some of the wild animals used in the gladiatorial games and to kill Christians were dinosaurs
4) Sea dragons (some able to breath fire) were also real since God moves on from describing the real behemoth in Job 40 to describing Leviathan in Job 41 with no indication that God has switched to describing mythical creatures

CHAPTER EIGHT

Things With Wings

"All that glisters; is not gold" says Shakespeare's play. Likewise: Everything with wings: Is not a bird! Let us go back to day five of the Creation week to see what else God created besides fish, sea monsters and plankton. God also made things with wings—the 'owph'—on that day.

The Hebrew word for the type of life that flies in the open firmament or atmosphere is typified by the physical feature known as wings. Do birds have wings? Yes. Do bats have wings? Yes. Do Pterodactyls have wings? Yes! Do dragonflies have wings? Yes. Do supposedly 'mythical' dragons that fly have wings? Yes! (More on this later!) In Genesis 1:20; God only said that He made things with wings. There are other words in the Hebrew language that mean birds or types of birds (though some of these may also be misinterpreted; such as tsippowr and yownah). At this point; God is only outlining the major classes of life that He created on given days.

God's classification system for animals seems to be quite different from the one we learned where the animal kingdom was divided into mammals, fish, birds, reptiles and amphibians. That system of classification was invented in the 1800s. A close look at God's system of classification reveals that: **He did not attend an American high school!** He uses a much simpler way: Living things in the sea; Living things that fly in the sky; and: Living things on the land. Of the things that live in the sea; God further breaks them into: fishes, swarming things {plankton / krill} and sea monsters. Of the things that live on land; He breaks them into: Behemoth (large quadrupeds), creeping things (small and fast), beasts of the earth (in between the other two). Leave it to God to keep it simple for we mere mortals.

It is *our method* of classifying critters that has been highjacked by satan to lead us to some misconceptions of the Bible! God is not the One that is confused! Remember! One MUST understand the Scripture from the cultural and historical times and in the language it was written!! Ken Ham, the founder of the wonderful Answers in Genesis ministry—which, by the way, is building a full size Ark of Noah; check their website because YOU can help with this project!—anyway, Ken Ham tells the story of some miscommunications that occurred because he was Australian when first in America—though both countries use English as a primary language.

An Australian friend of his had his car battery die. He went to get a new one and told the clerk, "My car battery is flat—I need a new one." The clerk looked quizzically at him and after they had figured out the problem said, "I thought you meant you had run over your battery!" Another friend of theirs had a new baby and the mother was known to breast feed. She needed to take a trip to the ladies room and asked her new female American friend, "Would you nurse my baby for a bit?" The woman stared at her until they figured out that the new mother only meant, "Would you hold / watch / care for my baby for a little while."

If such misunderstanding can happen in slightly different countries that DO speak the same language and have basically the same culture— can you see that there may be some misunderstandings when going from ancient cultures where kings ruled with absolute authority; to elected and power-split congresses or parliaments that are supposed to listen to and act on the people's desires?

Once a misunderstanding is detected; it may be able to be cleared up. This is what needs to be done with ALL the animal references in the English Bible—though my research indicates that WE will be in for quite a shock at what such a study will reveal. I believe I have only scratched the surface and led the way to a horde of clay jars that contain a treasure trove of information—if we will lose our evolutionary preconceptions drilled into us by the priests of the evolution religion. It may well be that men rode on and fought from flying creatures we would call dragons as is so often portrayed in movies like The Lord of the Rings and Eragon!

In this chapter we want to look at things that fly in the air. The fossil record shows us that large flying reptiles once lived and credible reports from remote places around the world indicate they quite likely still do live. The fossil record also shows us that: Birds have always been birds, Bats have always been bats; and: Pterodactyls have always been Pterodactyls. Bird fossils have been found in rock layers with and even below dinosaur fossils—so those evolutionists that claim dinosaurs turned into birds are either ignorant (bad) or deliberately lying (worse).

The word in Hebrew translated as fowl or fowls is: Owph—and means simply "having a wing or wings, covered with wings / feathers" according to Strong's. The word DOES NOT require feathers to be present; but does not rule feathers out either.

Were owph {fowls} taken on the Ark with Noah? Yes! Fowls are specifically mentioned and even if they were not: The all-encompassing Hebrew word for air breathing, living thing {chay} is used to describe the critters that came to Noah to be saved alive. It therefore follows that some flying lizards after being released from the Ark may have survived to the present time. There are stories by Christian missionaries—widely believed to be the most honest of human beings—of Pterosaurs of various types from around the world. Many times these stories from Africa include the eerie habit of these creatures eating human flesh from corpses if a body is not buried deeply enough. Now that sounds like the accounts and prophecies of battle dead being feasted on when God calls the beasts of the field and fowls of the air to gorge on the flesh of the defeated enemies of God. Certainly vultures would fit the bill, but why could not Pterosaurs as well?

Could that invitation to eat those killed in battle include flying dragons? Those things are just legends; right? What if I were to show you **the writings of Moses that identify them?** Turn to Leviticus chapter 11. In this chapter; Moses outlines those types of animals that the Israelites may and may not eat. In English; the list calls out some 40 different specific creatures that may or may not be eaten. In English, there seems to be no rhyme or reason to the list. Many have tried to make sense of it and find some pattern; such as for health reasons. No pattern really fits them all—until now!

Each of the critters mentioned in English is a specific creature such as a stork. An English speaking person reads the word and immediately forms a picture of the animal in their mind. If you look up each animal in Strong's you immediately find that only FOUR are somewhat specific creatures in the Hebrew language and those four **are all insects!** All the others are descriptive terms of some characteristic of the animal—a distinctive body part such as a claw or something they do, such as lacerate their prey—which is typical for the Hebrew culture as pointed out earlier in this book.

For example; in English we read the word 'eagle'—did not your American brain immediately download an image of our national symbol: The Bald Eagle? In Hebrew; the word we read as eagle is actually the word meaning, 'to lacerate or one that lacerates'. Obviously this creature has sharp claws and / or teeth. It is found in a sub-list of owph—other creatures that apparently fly or at least have wings. The translators in 1611 made the jump (transliteration as opposed to translation—necessary at times) to eagle in English— apparently because eagles lacerate their prey today and they were familiar with eagles while probably not familiar with flying dragons except in legends. It could just as easily be some type of Pterosaur or flying dragon if; of course; one is willing to set aside the 'millions of years' and 'no man ever saw a dinosaur' dogmas of the evolution religion.

Another example from Leviticus 11 is the English word tortoise. The Hebrew simply means "canopy or has a canopy". The translators transliterated this word to tortoise. This is strange because the tortoise is part of a sub-list that is said to include only beasts (behema—large quadrupeds)! Yes; the Galapagos Island tortoises are big and slow, but fall well short of what we have already come to see as true behema—and were UNKNOWN to the 1611 translators!! They were discovered by ocean explorers and studied by good ol' Charlie Darwin in the mid-1800s. The ONLY creatures they knew as having a canopy were the European or Asian tortoises—so that is what they decided on. Is it possible that Moses was actually describing an Anklyosaurus? Now that would be a canopied behema!—very large, four-legged and a tree-like tail. Or maybe he meant a Triceratops with its famous canopy. I lean toward Anklyosaurus because one of the Psalms describes a creature known as the Ox-Bullock that fits the Triceratops better (now you have to read on to that part, huh?).

In fact; many of the animals mentioned could have just as easily been transliterated into a reptilian creature that we today think of as dinosaurs. For example; the words translated as mouse and weasel also can be translated as types of lizards according to Strong's. A very coherent pattern emerges if this chapter is read with dinosaurs and large lizards in mind rather than the hodgepodge of animals the English speaking readers would be familiar with. Why would God be so negative towards reptiles? Well; recall that it was a serpent (still possessing legs) that allowed satan to use him to deceive our first parents Adam and Eve. That Fall condemned the human race and all creation to suffering and death that was otherwise unknown. That would be sufficient reason to be just a little negative towards this segment of the animal kingdom. However, the real reason is that God needed to label some critters unclean and some clean for a much greater reason as a future chapter details.

Did I say a flying dragon earlier? Sure, why not? Moses writes a little further in the list of Leviticus 11 at verse 22—25 about eating "flying creeping things that go on all fours". Then he clarifies for two verses that it is OK to eat what are apparently types of grasshoppers or in one case a type of beetle. These are the only four critters pretty specifically known to be in English what they were in Hebrew in all of Leviticus 11. In that clarification; he uses specific Hebrew words that have pretty specific English translations. There is little or no transliteration here— when Moses says grasshopper or locust; he means just that or at least some type of insect. People do in fact eat these and other insects today in many parts of the world.

How could anyone mistake a grasshopper for a flying dragon? The fossil record does contain grasshoppers two feet long that would have weighed about two pounds! After the clarification; he returns to his theme that the people are not to eat "flying creeping things that have four feet". As discussed before; creeping things were the small skittery critters—when the general Hebrew term is used. There is another Hebrew word that is translated creeping thing / creepeth / etc. that can only be used in the context of describing a reptile or the activities of a reptile. Apparently these were actual creatures that may have looked a lot like the little flying dragon in the Disney movie <u>Mulan</u>. Do humans eat lizards and snakes anywhere on earth—yes, they do.

I didn't write Leviticus; God through Moses did. I am only telling you what the best expert of ancient languages says the words mean. Moses here describes a creature that is of the smaller size (relative to a full-size dragon); has four feet and can fly (or at least has wings). Birds have only two legs and feet. The only other choices of things that fly and have four feet are: Pegasus the flying horse; the Piasa bird of American Indian legend; or the flying dragons of legends the world over. Take your pick.

Pegasus would have had hooves and there is a Hebrew word for hoof / hooves not used here—it appears the legendary flying horse is a non-candidate. The Piasa Bird found in American Indian lore does fit well. It was a flying creature with four feet about the size of a horse and it had a nearly human face. The other choice is the flying dragon of which there are many legends. Many times it has been found that legends usually are poor or distorted memories of real events / creatures. We have also observed FROM SCRIPTURE that the sea monster Leviathan probably had more than one head and spit fire—making the legends closer to truth than we have been willing to believe.

One other possibility is that Moses was still speaking of grasshoppers. There is a problem with this interpretation in addition to the problem previously discussed. Moses emphasizes to the people that: Not only are they not to eat these things—they are not even to touch their dead bodies. The word used for the dead body of these critters is translated into the English word 'carcass' but in Hebrew means 'flabby thing'. How many grasshoppers do you know of that have a flabby body? None! Grasshoppers have exoskeletons; not flesh. When they die, they dry out quickly and become crunchy. I have squished plenty of them—living and dead (hey, I was a boy, okay?)—from many different species including locusts—the word 'flabby' never came to mind; 'gooey'—yes; 'flabby'—no. Moses has clearly transitioned away from insects back to behema type creatures.

The following section details each English word for each animal named and gives the Hebrew word either transliterated or translated with the definitions from Strong's. You will note that some of the English names do not even fit the characteristic the assigned English 'bird' is supposed to exhibit. In other places; the guess by the transliterator /

translator identifies a completely different 'bird' than is assigned to the 'bird' listed in Scripture! That list starts with the fowls in verse 13—identifications that are essentially guesses by Strong's are found in {}.

- Eagle   to lacerate
- Ossifrage   a claw {a type of eagle}
- Osprey   from the word strength {probably a sea-eagle}
- Vulture   primary root "to dart" {the kite}
- Kite   the screamer {hawk or vulture}
- Raven   from the root "to be darkened or grow dusky"
- Owl   no actual translation root or word indicated by Strong's
- Night hawk   from root, "to be violent", {owl}
- Cuckow   from root, "to peel", emaciate
- Hawk   from root, "to be bright colored", flashing speed
- Little   owl to hold together, {owl}
- Cormorant   casting into the sea, {pelican}
- Great   owl from word 'to blow', {heron, perhaps night heron}
- Swan   tanshemeth (root word tan) hard breather, {mole / swan}
- Pelican   from vomiting {cormorant}
- Gier   eagle a kind of {vulture}, supposed to be tender toward its young
- Stork   the kind bird
- Heron   to breathe hard, unclean bird, {perhaps the parrot}
- Lapwing   of uncertain derivation, {hoopoe or grouse}
- Bat   of uncertain derivation, {bat}

After reading the definitions from Strong's; one gets the distinct idea that in making this list of things that have wings and / or fly—the translators did the best they could in their day with the understanding and life experiences that they had; just like any translator does today. However, according to other sections of Scripture with which this section MUST agree; these critters are supposed to also feast on dead bodies—the Owl, Cuckow, Little Owl, Comorant, Great Owl, Swan, Pelican, Stork, Heron, Lapwing and Bat have never been observed exhibiting this type of behavior to my knowledge. I could see perhaps the Owls and Bat might join the feast, but that still leaves several other critters from the list that have NEVER been observed exhibiting this behavior.

As previously noted, my great grandfather was the pastor of the Pilgrims. His name was Reverend John Robinson—and he is quoted as advising those departing for the New World that God has yet to reveal more truth and that they should be ready to embrace it. Perhaps this is why I was open to what seems an impossibly fantastic story when so many others would not be—maybe it is in my genes. At any rate, the consistent Hebrew pattern seems to be to describe what the animal does or a distinguishing feature of that animal. The English culture puts a definite name to a particular animal.

If you were faced with the same translation dilemma—bridging the gap between decidedly different cultures—how would you handle it? Would you have put in the matching word for word description {translate}; knowing your audience would have little chance of understanding because of cultural differences—or would you have decided to take your best guess {transliterate} and give the critter a known name consistent with your culture? The translators apparently prayed and were led to the latter course of action. Again the Bible is 100% accurate in its ORIGINAL language as understood in it original CULTURAL context.

It should be obvious by now that there is no real substitute for knowing Hebrew and Greek {and those cultures} if you wish to truly understand the Bible. This is why there are so many 'translations' into English today—some good and some quite awful in my too often not so humble opinion. Part of the reason there is so much Biblical heresy today regarding so many topics is that some 'translators' simply put their pet ideas into the text where clearly nothing of the sort is actually there. Some may accuse me of that very thing in this work; but my work goes back to the original words and their best available translations / transliterations. This is not me making up stuff out of thin air as many have; all I do in this work is draw consistent conclusions from the existing, accepted work that has been used for more than a hundred years—Strong's Exhaustive Concordance!

If you do not know Hebrew and Greek—your only alternative is to ally yourself with a trustworthy church and pastors who do. I have—and I have studied enough of the languages to be able to use a Strong's effectively. I now refuse to take a stand on any topic until I have researched it in the original language and tried to understand it from the original culture. If Christians would take a step back and do the same before allowing satan to divide them (satan knows Scripture better than we do!)—many church splits could be avoided. However, even church splits often result in the further spread of God's Word—so satan is defeated again, even in his temporary 'victory' in stopping some particular mission.

From the aforementioned list is one clue; that at least one of the animals named is what we would call a type of Pterosaur—found in the definition for the flying creature identified in English as the swan. The actual word is: Tanshemeth—the root word being 'tan' which means to elongate or monster. Tan is also the root word for 'tanniyn'—the land dwelling dragon or sea monster. This fact should be enough to lead even a skeptic to at least the suspicion that this creature in the list of things with wings is a flying reptile!

Let us go back to verse 20 of chapter 11 for a moment—to emphasize one point more clearly. Moses describes a very strange (impossible actually) characteristic of these flying animals if he was speaking of what we would understand to be birds, "All fowls that creep (sherets-wiggle / swarm), going upon all fours . . ." What on earth? A bird that wiggles / swarms and goes upon all fours? Or did Moses really mean; a flying thing or thing with wings that also wiggles / swarms and goes upon all fours? Again; Hebrew scholars: Here is a book just waiting to be written! Get to it! It will take me 20 years to get to where you are, if I ever do—and the body of Christ cannot wait that long.

To make matters worse; God through Moses then says in verse 21&22, "{21} Yet these may ye eat of every flying creeping thing that goeth upon all four, *which have legs above their feet, to leap withal upon the earth*; {22} Even these of them ye may eat; the locust (grass-hopper / locust-definitely identified) after his kind, and the bald locust (a kind of locust—from its destructiveness) after his kind, and the beetle (leaping insect—locust) after his kind, and the grasshopper (uncertain derivation—a locust) after his kind." The critters are more definitely described than the other things with wings and much more consistent with the words "legs above their feet, to leap withal upon the earth". Notice also that these creatures are not described as creeping things.

To illustrate the point of the difficulty of language translation further; consider that this same section reads in the Geneva Bible as: "{22} Of them shall ye eat these, the grasshopper after his kind, and the solean after his kind, the hargol after his kind, and the hagab after his kind." What?! Three of the four words are from old English—that would have been clear to the people of the 1550 A.D. timeframe, but not today. Do you see why I believe far less than 40% of the animals named with specific English names in today's language are really that animal in the pages of Scripture?

Now after clarifying that it is okay to eat some kinds of insects that otherwise could be mistaken for forbidden kinds of critters; God through Moses returns to speaking of the animals that the Israelites may not eat. We can infer this because he again says the unclean critters are those that creep (swarm), "{23} But all other flying creeping things, which have four feet, shall be an abomination unto you." Now these creatures that in verse 20 went about on all fours are further identified as having four feet! The word feet means, "a foot (as used in walking)"! I cannot strongly enough point out that God says these creatures would be considered to have a 'carcass (flabby thing)' and that grasshoppers; even big ones—could not be considered to have flabby bodies. In the Geneva Bible it reads with the words in italics removed because they are not really there in the original Greek text, "{23} But all fowls that creep; have four feet—they: An abomination unto you."

Be honest now—even you evolutionist skeptics reading this book to find some way to discredit me and / or doubt God: If you were on a game show like the old $100,000 Pyramid where one contestant says words and you had to guess what the topic was: What would you say if your partner gave you the same clues Moses gives us? Here are the clues: Flying thing—Has four feet—Is not a locust—Wiggles and swarms—It has carcass described as flabby. No one on earth would conclude that Moses was talking about some kind of known bird! The only guesses people would venture would be perhaps bats, but; no—they do not have four feet. Hmmm . . . . Dragons?—but those are only the stuff of myths . . . Right?

Moses is the writer here for God and neither of them gives any indication they are telling the Israelites that they may not eat mythical creatures. Moses is clearly speaking about real animals that his readers would readily be able to identify from the information given IN THEIR DAY and IN THEIR CULTURE—not ours! Moses was dictating the Laws of God from God!—he was not writing some fanciful trilogy like <u>Dune</u>.

Summary of main points:

1) During creation week, God made things with wings—the owph—which included flying animals of all sorts, not just birds
2) Some of these creatures were considered unclean, but not all—since the Levitical law identifies the unclean ones, inferring that all the others are clean
3) Moses identifies creatures that logically were dragons

CHAPTER NINE

Peter's Vision

Remember the dictionary entries cited several pages ago? Dragons were "rare but still living creatures" in the 1700s before the false religion of evolution invented the doctrine of 'millions and billions of years ago' and 'no man has ever seen a dinosaur' . . . Even after 60 years of evolutionary indoctrination (1880s—1940s)—the 1940s vintage dictionary I own says dragons are "rare" but does not deny that they actually were still living. It was only after nearly 100 years of brainwashing the population in public school (1880s to 1980s) that dragons could finally be *redefined* as "mythical" creatures. Now with a resurgence of creationist thought; people are once again questioning the millions / billions of years jargon and becoming open to the possibility of man living with creatures we would call dinosaurs in the historical past.

Speaking of history—the word 'prehistoric' is also a recent entrant into our language. That same English dictionary from the 1700s DOES NOT have the word prehistoric in it! Up until the lying doctrine of evolution came into prominence—people believed there was only History—recorded in the pages of the Bible! If you doubt that as recently as 1802 the prevailing view was that of the Bible being historically accurate—as I previously said; get a copy of Knickerbocker's <u>History of New York</u>. This satirical writer spends a long opening chapter discussing the various origins theories concocted by man.

He quotes Darwin's theory of the origin of the solar system—but not Charles Darwin; he quotes Erasmus Darwin! Erasmus Darwin appears to have been Charles Darwin's grandfather or great uncle—and likely was the one who filled young Charles' mind with the poison that would spawn <u>On the Origin of Species</u> a few decades later. The author openly mocks **ALL** the ideas—including Darwin's—conjured up from all over the world—and concludes the chapter by saying that until someone comes up with something that makes sense: He would stick with the account of Moses in the Bible.

Just because Moses is speaking of animals we are not familiar with today; because very few have ever seen them—certainly DOES NOT mean they never existed. People in western nations never saw a Coelacanth except in fossil form until 1938 when they were found to be a fairly common catch in the Indian Ocean. What did the evolutionists have to say about these critters they had confidently said were extinct for 70 million years? Why—they were amazed that these lobe finned fish had not changed while the rest of the world's animals, including man had supposedly changed so much! Evolutionists simply cannot admit that their evolution religion is a completely wrong interpretation of a selected portion of the evidence available; that has actually been woven into a religion—upon which altar these otherwise intelligent and reasonably honest people have sacrificed their reason and objective intellect. It is evolution that is the myth; not the accounts of man living with dinosaurs, then called dragons.

Why do evolutionists get to rethink their debunked ideas while still proclaiming their disproved ones as indisputable fact? Creation believing persons who have never been proved wrong are afforded no such luxury and lambasted on a regular basis! The only reasonable explanation for this is the existence of a being able to blind men's minds to the Truth. That being is satan—according to Jesus Christ; satan is a liar and the father of lies. Jesus said satan was a murderer from the beginning and that when he lies he speaks his native tongue!

This sinister being is good at what he does: He got Adam and Eve to turn over the title to the entire earth to him! Every lying politician or con-man has studied in his school! Our first parents did not have to have a job or worry about food or shelter. They had actual fellowship with God and were immortal. There was no need for any type of government—or taxes—or; for that matter; money. Yes—all this was traded away for: A LIE—and all that came with it: Death, oppression; sickness; separation from God; war; crime; worry; the IRS and Federal Reserve; etc.; etc.; etc.!

Today—this liar has blinded the minds of otherwise intelligent and good people. When a person such as myself confronts them with indisputable evidence that they are wrong—they usually walk away or begin to hurl nasty insults. They lock those who dare challenge them out of universities and prestigious 'science' organizations. They too often are elected to school boards so they can control the curriculum and continue the brain-washing of our children. They control much of the major media and again shut out or set up to embarrass any who dare take them on. We indeed are battling against ' . . . wickedness in high places." as Paul told us in his letter to the Ephesians.

The interesting part is: They are still losing the Culture War!! Over 85% of Americans still believe in some form of creation—albeit many ignorantly and subconsciously mix evolution and creation—as I used to do. This view is called Theistic Evolution: God did it but used evolution to do it. It is the majority view in America today; probably close to 50% of Americans ascribe to it. Still—the true evolutionist; who by definition must be an Atheist—accounts for 5% of the population at most. The tail truly wags the dog in American public school Science classrooms and too often in American politics where Charles Darwin's atheistic dogmas are regarded as fact. Notice that Republican / Conservative Presidential candidates are routinely asked mockingly if they believe in Creationism—while Democrats are never mockingly asked WHY they believe evolution when this belief system is provably WRONG!!

There can be only one explanation for the evolutionists losing: God is on our side! God cares for the Truth and ensures people who desire the Truth get to hear it! Hear the words of Paul's first letter to Timothy at chapter 2 verses 3—6 paraphrased: "This is good and pleases God our Saviour; Who wants all men to be saved and come to knowledge of the Truth—for there is one God and one Mediator between God and men—the Man; Christ Jesus—Who gave Himself as a ransom for all men." God defends those who stand for His Word! He turns the wisdom of those who are wise in their own eyes into foolishness. I heard Christian speaker Frank Paretti say once, "Yes, boys and girls: Nothing exploded—then turned into goo—then turned into you—by way of the zoo!!" He did an excellent job of boiling down the nonsense that is evolutionary musing into a one-liner.

The tragic part is what is coming next in the LIE that is evolutionary 'thinking': 'The next step boys and girls: You evolve into gods!' God will not share His glory with anyone! He will not share it with satan—or any fool that follows satan. He will not share His Glory with you, either. Wise up! Believe God and His Word! This means your sin—as a Gentile believer—must be cleansed somehow. This is where the New Testament—drawing from the Old Testament—comes into play with Peter's vision.

In Leviticus 11—look at the list in verses 26 & 27—while remembering all we have learned so far about this list. God through Moses addresses "{11:26} the carcasses of every beast (behema-large quadruped) which divide the hoof, and is not clovenfooted, nor cheweth the cud, are unclean . . . {27} And whatsoever goeth upon his paws, among all manner of beasts (chay-living thing) . . ." Moses finishes for a time speaking about large creatures and moves on to the smaller ones in verses 29 through 38. God through Moses begins with "{11:29} . . . unclean unto you among the creeping things that creep upon the earth . . . :

- Weasel   from root meaning to glide swiftly
- Mouse   probably from same root meaning attacking
- Tortoise   from the root meaning to establish, covered, a type of lizard
- Ferret   some kind of lizard, from a root meaning shriek
- Chameleon   to be firm, vigor, a large lizard
- Lizard   from root meaning to hide, a lizard
- Snail   from root meaning to lie low, a lizard, as creeping
- Mole   tanshemeth (yup! Same word as swan!) a hard breather

Are you getting the same feeling that I am? The translators again chose real English animals as transliterations for Hebrew words that are only characteristics—just like they did for the list of supposed birds! In each case; the animal is really not identifiable for those of us who did not live in that DAY and CULTURE—but certainly all could be reptiles those people were very familiar with!

Now just for an instant; let yourself be Moses. This man is a very orderly and logical thinker. God is dictating laws to him and is not playing games. Moses would be very consistent; very logical; very sensible in this task. Does it really make sense that he would swerve around the animal kingdom the way these lists do in English? Would it not make better sense if each of these animals being described were from the same basic kind of animal—and there was some kind of connection to the concept that God introduced: clean and unclean? Each of these wiggly, swarming things could have been identified as some sort of lizard or reptile. Each of the things with wings could describe any number of flying things with the 'swan' almost certainly being a flying monster. These things with wings like a pterodactyl when grounded would crawl on all fours like bats do when they hit the ground; two wings and two feet. The other flying creeping things that have four feet could be dragons; they fly and most often have four feet in every legend or movie I have read or seen.

Why wouldn't God be quite angry with this specific group of animals in the animal kingdom? It was a beast of the field—specifically the nachash before losing its legs—that was possessed of satan to deceive the first man and woman. The beasts of the field were not necessarily the behema but may have been a type of behemoth depending on how Genesis 3:14 is understood. I believe Leviticus chapter 11 is chock full of dinosaurs from beginning to end! Before you shake your head in disbelief; take a look at the New Testament! The Bible must be consistent in both New and Old Testaments; for God—the Author—changes not! Also; the Law and the sacrificial system had not accomplished permanent salvation, even for the Jews—it only made men know they were sinners. Worse; most of humanity was outside even the limited atonement afforded by the Law of the Jews.

What can be done? Has God failed in His mission to save fallen man from himself? Will only a few Jews be saved and the rest of mankind be condemned? Or—has God had a Master Plan all along!—has God fooled satan into carrying out His plan of offering salvation to the entire world; once for all—never needing to be repeated? Many have wondered if One Mind penned all of Scripture or if the Bible is only a rather odd collection of stories pieced together with much of it made up or stylized. The next few paragraphs show that God did write the entire Bible—for our salvation if we believe on His Son Jesus Christ!

Turn to Acts chapter 10:10-15 for a look at the vision given to Peter with Scripture in bold and my notes not bolded, **"{10} And he**

(Peter) **became very hungry, and would have eaten: but while they made ready, he fell into a trance!—{11} and saw heaven opened!—and a certain vessel descending unto him; as it had been a great sheet knit at the four corners and let down to the earth: {12} Wherein were all manner of fourfooted beasts** (Greek-four footed) **of the earth, and wild beasts** (therion—root word thera—a dangerous or venomous animal), **and creeping things** (herpeton—a reptile, creeping thing, serpent), **and fowls** (a flying animal) **of the air. {13} And there came a voice to him, 'Rise, Peter! Kill and eat!' {14} But Peter said, 'Not so, Lord!—for I have never eaten any thing that is common** (shared by all—unclean) **or unclean** (foul / demonic).' **{15} And the voice spake unto him again the second time, 'What God hath cleansed** (Greek-purge, purify); **that: Call thou not common** (called or regarded as common).'"

Notice that the Greek is indistinct for each type of animal and so is the English. We get one clue in that: The Greek word transliterated as 'wild beasts' is the word therion with a root word thera. Therapsida is defined in Webster's 9th Collegiate Dictionary as, "(from Greek theraps) any of an order of Permian and Triassic reptiles . . ." Another clue is found in the Greek word for creeping things; herpeton—with the root word herpe. Herpetology is today: The study of reptiles!

Peter describes all the critters he has seen as 'common'; the Greek word implies that all have the same characteristics—all are unclean; perhaps he also means all are reptiles as well. God doesn't correct him outright, but uses a slightly different word for common meaning '**called** common or **regarded as** unclean'—reminding Peter that <u>He was the One</u> back in Noah's time that designated certain animals unclean. Peter was a Jew! He was raised on the Law of Moses! There was no book called the 'New Testament' yet!—because he was living some of the experiences that would become the New Testament!

Certainly a Jew would have looked back at the creatures Moses called unclean in the book of the Laws of the Jewish Nation—Leviticus! Out of the entire book of Leviticus; it is chapter 11 that contains the lists of animals; behema—large quadrupeds, beasts of the earth, creeping things and fowls that are unclean!!! He would have known the Jewish culture much better than we Gentiles or even modern Jews do today. These words which are somewhat unclear to us—were obviously very clear to Peter! He knew exactly what critters God was showing him in this vision.

Two of the four types of animals identified in Acts 10 are definitely reptiles, a third type is / are large quadruped(s) and the fourth is 'flying animals' {not specifically a bird}. The vision was of unclean animals let down to the earth; so it is not surprising that the unclean swimming creatures are omitted; though they are found in Leviticus 11. All share the same characteristics of being unclean as declared by God to Noah, the account recorded by Moses. All of the creatures in Leviticus are either clean or are / could be reptiles. Not all of the reptiles in Leviticus are unclean. Some are clean as demonstrated by Noah taking clean behema aboard the Ark by sevens and offering clean behema as a burnt sacrifice after departing the Ark. The unclean behema and beasts of the earth also were taken aboard. Now God is calling all these creatures cleansed or purged or purified!

This vision happened three times to emphasize its importance. Peter uses the vision's analogy to break down the millennia old barrier of Jew (clean-holy) to Gentile (unclean-heathen). Only a very significant; spiritually representative example of God purifying all unclean animals—that has for literally the entire existence of the Jewish nation (actually for hundreds of years before the Jewish nation existed!) symbolized something not to be so much as touched—would cause Peter to even consider breaking the Law of non-association with Gentiles.

Now suddenly these critters are declared clean by the only One Who could—the One Who declared them unclean in the first place!—now they are clean / acceptable!—and can even be eaten without imputing uncleanness to oneself! Why?—because God has done the purifying! God made Peter understand that He has also purified believing Gentiles who come to Him through faith in Jesus Christ's redeeming Blood! There is to be no difference between a saved Jew and a saved Gentile! Thank God for me—an otherwise unclean Gentile—now a fully purified Christian believer! Over 99% of all the people in the world are not Jews!

Peter obviously understands that God has accepted the Gentiles—because He has cleansed those who believe on the Lord Jesus Christ for forgiveness of sins. He immediately puts the vision's message into actual practice by going to and into the house of a heathen Roman centurion: Cornelius. This was a very serious violation of the Jewish Law! Recall from Scripture that even in their hast to get Jesus condemned by Pilate—the Jewish leaders would not enter into the Gentile Roman leader Pilate's home, but forced him to come out to them. Peter then preaches to these Gentiles and the Spirit of God comes upon the new Gentile believers just as it had on the first Jewish believers at Pentecost and the half-Jew Samaritans a short time later in Acts. God has indeed cleansed and in-grafted all true believers into the same family tree!

There can be no doubt that One Mind authored all of Scripture! Here is a subplot so intricate—that it apparently was not even detected by the human writers of Scripture themselves! God simply and arbitrarily declares certain animals clean and unclean to Noah because He is God and can do such a thing. Noah doesn't question the proclamation—neither does he ask for an explanation. Noah does not indicate that he understands why God has done it: He simply obeys. None of the writers of any of the books of the Old Testament give any hint whatever that they understand why God has declared some animals unclean and clean. It is not even a point of discussion in the Bible. God kept it as a secret for more than 2500 years until Peter is given a vision that can only be understood to mean that God's grace is so powerful that it has opened the door for all men through the work of Jesus on the Cross! Again from Scripture; Romans 10:4 'Christ is the end of the Law—so that there may be Righteousness for everyone who believes!' Only an unseen Hand penning this supremely mysterious subplot over centuries and through many human authors can explain such consistency of purpose and thought! God wrote the Bible through obedient human beings!!!

It is probable that the reptiles were chosen for this dubious distinction of being unclean because one of their kind was possessed of satan and tempted God's pinnacle of creation; Adam and Eve. The grand plan of God was to arbitrarily discriminate against these animals and regard them with loathing as a symbol of that which is separated from God. Then; after Jesus pays the price for sin—the curse is lifted and all may be regarded as holy again; with the obvious understanding that it is by the declaration of God that the unclean has been made clean! God declares sinners who repent to no longer be unclean requiring separation from God—but rather as members of His family! This declaration is ONLY applied to those who accept forgiveness of sins by faith in the Lord Jesus Christ.

Have YOU become a member of God's family? Why not do it right now!

Are you a sinner? Yes. Is there a sinless human substitute that can pay your sin-debt (because you cannot, having admitted you are a sinner)? Yes!—the only 'God-man'; Jesus Christ. Do you want Him to pay your debt for you?—or would you rather party with satan for eternity in Hell?

I am going to go out on a limb here and guess that you want to go to Heaven. Then just ask King Jesus to forgive your sin-debt. He will. It is really as easy as that. Just remember, you have now given your life to the King—and the Holy Spirit will wage war for control of your life. If you fight this process—it will not be pretty. Please, do not fight Him—you will not win. I fought Him for the first few years—and from time to time afterwards. I lost every time. Join a Bible believing church and find some new friends—your old ones will not really miss you that much.

Summary of main points:

1) The reason for clean and unclean is made clear—as an example of God's ability to declare forgiveness of sins for anyone, Jew or Gentile
2) There appears to be an effort to redefine dragons from real creatures into mythical ones—the only purpose would be to protect the false evolutionary doctrine of 'no man with dinosaurs'
3) A similar effort is apparent to undermine the Bible as History—by adding the word pre-historic to the English language—the only purpose for this would be to lend credibility to the evolution religion

4) The topic of clean and unclean—involving dinosaurs—spans from the Creation week to after Jesus death and resurrection: Clearly One Mind authored all Scripture!

5) Pardon for your sin is a paid-for-by-Someone-else gift! John 3:14-16 shows the evil nachash (satan inhabiting a type of behemoth) was lifted up in the wilderness for the sin-infected Jews to be saved from a plague—and Jesus was lifted up for us in our day so that we may be saved from sin.

CHAPTER TEN

The Rest of the New Testament

Since we are now into the New Testament; let us explore the animals featured in its pages besides the references in Acts 10. In Peter's vision; the term 'wild beasts' was used and found to be the word therion in Greek. The first time the word therion appears is in Mark 1:13 where Jesus is in the wilderness after His baptism, **"And He was there in the wilderness forty days tempted of Satan—and was with the wild beasts (therion); and the angels ministered to Him."** Notice the close association of unclean reptiles with satan; just like in the Garden of Eden account! Is this a replay of history? Adam fell to nachash's hissing lie. Nachash still had his legs at that time and was certainly a reptile. The Garden was paradise and Adam lost it. Now because of sin; the Garden is a wilderness!—and Christ has come to conquer satan to regain paradise! Once again, reptiles associated with satan are present.

Most of us have heard that Christians were forced to entertain Romans by fighting lions in arenas; but is that what Scripture really says? Paul tells us of his time in the arena at Ephesus in 1 Corinthians 15:32, **"If after the manner of men I have fought with beasts (theriomacheo-wild beast fighter in a gladiator show) at Ephesus, what advantage it me, if the dead rise not? Let us eat and drink, for to morrow we die."** Paul is arguing the point of his faith in life after death. The words, "after the manner of men" indicates it was not unusual at all for people to fight against wild beasts (therion). WE assumed the wild beasts were always lions or tigers or bears (oh, my!).

Paul had another famous run in with a smaller therion after his famous shipwreck when he being transferred to Rome to stand trial before Caesar. Acts 28:3-5 tell us, "**{3} And when Paul had gathered a bundle of sticks, and laid them on the fire, there came a viper** (echidna-adder or other poisonous snake) **out of the heat, and**

fastened on his hand. {4} And when the barbarians saw the venomous beast (therion) **hang on his hand, they said among themselves, 'No doubt this man is a murderer!—whom; though he has escaped the sea—yet vengeance allows not to live.' {5} And he shook off the beast** (therion) **into the fire and felt no harm.**" The creature is identified as both a therion and an echidna in this passage. As Scripture cannot contradict itself; the echidna must be some type of therion—further strengthening the idea that a therion is a type of reptile.

John the Baptist and Jesus use the word echidna in their diatribes against the Pharisees. Matthew 3:7 and Luke 3:7 carry virtually identical accounts—so Matthew's rendering will be used here; "**{3:7} . . . O generation of vipers** (echidna)**! Who has warned you to flee from the wrath to come?**" Jesus says in Matthew 12:34, "**O generation of vipers** (echidna)**! How can you—being evil—speak good things?**" The next time Jesus is nearing the end of his famous indictment of the Scribes and Pharisees when He says in Matthew 23:33, "**You serpents** (ophis-sharp-eyed or sly one, often equated with satan)**! You generation of vipers** (echidna)**! How can you escape the damnation of hell?**" This entire class of animals has been associated with evil and uncleanness since the fall of man recorded in Genesis.

The word serpent appears many times in the New Testament and most often is the word ophis; meaning sharp-eyed or sly and very often is a synonym for satan. The first use is by Jesus in Matthew 7:10 (and it's parallel in Luke 11:11), "**{9} or what man is there of you; whom if his son ask bread—will give him a stone? {10} Or if he ask a fish; will he give him a serpent** (ophis)**?**" Matthew 10:16 records Jesus admonition to the disciples to be, "**wise as serpents** (ophis) **. . .**" The next is Mark 16:18, "**They shall take up serpents** (ophis) **. . .**" apparently indicating that disciples will have the ability to take on deadly doctrines of devils and not be harmed by them—it is possible He meant actual poisonous critters—or both meanings; since Paul battled heresy many times and suffered no ill effects of being bitten by the echidna type of therion feared by the island natives for its venom. This idea may be furthered by the verses in Luke 10:18&19 where Jesus gives authority over satan and his minions, "**{18} And He said to them, 'I beheld Satan as lightning fall from heaven. {19} Behold: I**

give to you power to tread on serpents (ophis) **and scorpions** (skorpios-piercing sting).'

Jesus then refers to the plague of fiery serpents put on the rebellious Israelites in the wilderness. The Gospel of John, third chapter, fourteenth through sixteenth verse has Jesus saying, **"{14} 'And as Moses lifted up the serpent** (ophis) **in the wilderness: Even so must the Son of man be lifted up: {15} That whosoever believe in Him should not perish; but have eternal life. {16} For God so loved the world that He gave His only begotten Son: That whosoever believes in Him should not perish but have everlasting life.'** "The most memorized verse in the New Testament is tied directly to a previous verse that has a reptile; possibly small dinosaur in it! The word for serpent in the Old Testament account to which Jesus referred is, are you ready: Seraph! Seraph means fiery and / or poisonous as well as copper colored serpent. Jesus was speaking to Nicodemas—a Jewish priest whose entire life had been dedicated to studying Scripture—he would have known if Jesus misquoted or misrepresented the Sacred Text.

Moses is told in Numbers 21:8 to make a fiery serpent (seraph) and set it upon a pole. Moses makes a serpent (nachash-the hissing one) and puts it on a pole. Remember that nachash is the serpent from the Garden of Eden that initiated the fall of man. If a man had been bitten by a serpent (nachash) here in the wilderness plague and looked upon the lifted up serpent (nachash) they would live. The implication is if any man bitten by sin (all of us) would look upon the crucified (lifted up) sin: He would not die; but live. Some two thousand years later; Jesus would become sin for us!—and be crucified (lifted up)! Anyone bitten by sin can look upon the crucified (dealt with) sin and not die, but live forever! The brass snake was only good for that one occasion for a relatively small group of persons. Jesus' payment is permanent and for the entire world!

The next time a serpent is referred to in the New Testament is again the word ophis in first and second Corinthians. We will only cover the account in 2 Corinthians 11:2&3, **"{2} For I am jealous over you with godly jealousy: for I have espoused you to one husband: That I may present you as a chaste virgin to Christ.**

{3} But I fear; less by any means as the serpent (ophis) **beguiled Eve through his subtilty . . ."** Paul is obviously referring to satan's inhabiting nachash in the Garden.

The final five references to ophis are all found in Revelation. John chooses the word ophis to describe satan in four of the five references. The first time is describing the snakelike tails of the armies of fallen angels of the bottomless pit. If this reference is not symbolic (which I believe most if not all of Revelation is symbolic like the dreams of Nebuchanezzar in Daniel); a new and terrible creature the likes of which have never been seen before will come forth from the pit of hell itself. The last four references are all clearly synonyms for satan.

Revelation 12:9, 14, 15 and 20:2 depict our ancient enemy. Revelation 12:9 reads, **"And the great dragon** (drakon-to look-a fabulous serpent supposed to fascintate)**, that old serpent** (ophis)**, called the Devil, and Satan . . ."** Revelation 12:14&15, **"{14} And to the woman were given two wings of a great eagle, that she might fly into the wilderness, into her place, where she is nourished for a time, and times, and half a time, from the face of the serpent** (ophis)**—{15} and the serpent** (ophis) **cast out of his mouth water as a flood after the woman: That he might cause her to be carried away of the flood."** The last time serpent is used is 20:1&2, **"{1} And I saw an angel come down from heaven; having the key of the bottomless pit and a great chain in his hand—{2} and he laid hold on the dragon** (drakon)**, that old serpent** (ophis)**, which is the Devil, and Satan, and bound him a thousand years."**

Paul further uses the word therion in describing the Cretans in Titus 1:12, **"a prophet of their own said, 'The Cretans are always liars!—evil beasts** (therion)**!—slow bellies!'"** Paul identifies evil with therion; certain types of reptiles. From the beginning, God has tied evil to the order of reptile that allowed satan to inhabit him.

There are other Greek words that could have been used such as the general term for a living thing—zoon. Paul, Peter and John did not use that word as associated with evil or uncleanness. Peter and Jude used zoon to describe brute or dumb, unthinking animals, but not as evil or wicked creatures. John used zoon many times in Revelation; always to describe the glorious creatures that surround the throne of God and give glory to Him with the elders.

In Revelation; John used therion as a contrasting term to identify the Beast that receives power and authority from the Dragon. From Revelation 11:7 to 20:10, John uses therion thirty-seven times as beast and once as beasts: Every use of therion is in context with satan or anti-Christ. John uses the word zoon twenty times: Every use in context with the living creatures that continually worship God and attend His throne. Clearly a spiritual message is indicated here. The type of animal that was possessed of Satan in the Garden has for all history been associated with evil—right through to the end of the Bible. Other animals of the reptile order fulfill their God ordained purpose of giving Him praise.

Only one other time is a Greek word rendered beasts in Revelation 18:3. It is the word ktenos and means domestic animal. In context; this is the appropriate word as the verse is speaking of other domesticated livestock such as sheep and horses. Clearly, John was very aware of his word choice options and chose exactly the word that best conveyed the meaning God intended him to convey. Therion were reptiles associated with satan in the New Testament; just as nachash was in the Old Testament.

The conclusion one must come to is that certain kinds of reptiles have been chosen by God to be associated with uncleanness, evil and satan. The physical representation of the spiritual evil being known as the devil is a type of reptile that fascinates; is sly or cunning; and has universally been regarded by man as the very symbol of evil.

Summary of main points:

1) Dinosaurs appear as mostly real animals in the Bible from beginning to end
2) Symbolically, some types of dinosaurs represent evil or are synonyms for satan
3) Other animals fulfill their God given role of praising Him!

CHAPTER ELEVEN

The 'OWR' Connection

It seems that Biblical references to dinosaurs may appear so frequently that a person searching the Scriptures for them is likely to miss the forest for the trees! Behema / behemoth is used about 190 times; tanniyn 27 times; eagles (one the lacerates) is used about 100 times; etc. We creationists would have been satisfied to find one clear reference to dinosaurs in the Bible. It turns out that there are so many references to odd creatures (in the original language) that really are dinosaurs that we may be unwilling to accept the obvious.

Dinosaurs were part of the creation that God spoke into existence. Man would not have taken exceptional note of the smaller ones any more we take note of dogs today or any more than any other creature that God had made. The only exception would be for the behemoth / behema which were so impressive and important to man's society and economic success of that era that they would be noted specially—just like man today takes special note of the Clydesdale horse or the St. Bernard dog while treating as nothing special all lesser types of horses and dogs. These animals would be a normal part of speech and regularly be included as appropriate to make a point or convey a message. It now appears we were looking so hard for a single specific reference to an animal that just might be a dinosaur that we overlooked the hundreds of times these creatures are mentioned.

Some of the references are not as clear as others—but evolutionists fly off on wild flings of fancy over a single bone fragment in the desert; building an entire person and story from it. To make this point in my lectures—I gathered up the dry remains of a road killed Persian cat that had wandered around our neighborhood for months. It had gotten fully dried out and decayed—so I put it in a clear plastic container. My kids could not believe it; especially when I told them I had named it

'Fluffy'. They are threatening to inter Fluffy's remains with me should my demise occur prior to Jesus' return.

My reason for doing such a thing—apart from entertaining teenage boys in the audience—was to ask a volunteer from the audience to come up and answer some questions about 'Fluffy'. I usually pick a squeamish girl for full effect—the more 'EEEWWWs!!!' evoked; the more entertainment value. Be sure of this—today's audiences DEMAND to be entertained if you want to keep their attention while making important points.

I start out by asking what type of animal it was and the volunteer gets this one right: It is obviously the remains of a cat. I then ask the person what it ate—they usually answer 'cat food'. I then ask if they know this or assume it because of their prior understanding of cats— they admit they do not and could not know what 'Fluffy' ate. I then ask if 'Fluffy' had any offspring—the person admits they do not know. I ask if 'Fluffy' had any mutant offspring—again they admit ignorance of 'Fluffy's' family. I ask about 'Fluffy's' living habits—they of course do not know. Asked about 'Fluffy's' demise—they say only an eyewitness could say for sure. Finally, I point out to the audience that ALL the STORIES about bones or teeth found in various places of the world are just speculations by those with a pre-existing belief system and possibly an agenda of convincing them the 'evolution religion' is true. Only God could have been an eyewitness to the events that resulted in the fossils being where they are—and He HAS given us an eye-witness account of His-story in the pages of Scripture: Noah's Flood.

So why cannot we believers in God's word be afforded a little leeway to speculate? The difference between myself and an evolutionist will be—when I speculate; I will tell you!—evolutionists try to convince you that their 'out-of-thin-air' stories are absolutely and unquestioningly true!

For the record; I am purely speculating for the rest of this chapter! If I am correct—and I do think that I am correct—there are hundreds more references to critters we would call dinosaurs in the pages of Scripture on top of the ones covered so far. In fact; the mammals many use for labor and travel in today's world would likely have been scoffed at when compared to the work ability and speed and carrying capacity of the critters possibly used by the peoples of the Old Testament. The greatest speculation I attempt here: Jesus Christ may have ridden into Jerusalem—as prophesied the Messiah would—on a dinosaur! Do I know that I am right? No! I was not there to see it happen. I can only analyze the words of Scripture.

I can be sure Christ DID ride into Jerusalem on some type of animal—DID die on the cross—DID rise from the dead—and CAN save me from my sins. These are basic DOCTRINES of Christianity. What kind of animal Jesus rode into Jerusalem on is NOT a DOCTRINE of Christianity—it is merely an interesting topic for dinner table discussion. If I am wrong on this point—so what? I am quite sure the evolutionists will pick this one short discussion out of the entire book to ridicule me about—oh, well. We will find out in heaven about all the various speculations fallible men have attempted over the centuries.

Here we go! The 'OWR' connection: Many animals that occur frequently in Scripture share the curious suffix (and in one case prefix) OWR. In my Strong's; it is word 5785 and is defined as 'skin (as naked)— by implication hide, leather, skin' and it is derived from a primary root word 5783 UWR which is defined as 'to (be) bare; be made naked'. The Chaldean equivalent is word 5784 UWR defined as 'chaff (as the naked husk)'. While these words do not absolutely rule out fur or short hair on the skin—these words do definitely seem to imply the absence of hair. Also; there are Hebrew words for hair and a hairy animal that is defined as 'shaggy'. If the Writer of Scripture (which ultimately is God through inspired men) wanted to send the message that the animal had hair; He easily could have. Why then, one must ask, did the Writer not specify this trait in a society where animals were described by their traits?

There is another OWR found in Scripture as well. The word 216-owr means 'lightning' and is derived from 215-owr-luminous, set on fire. The dragon legends of old speak of fire associated with these critters. Lucifer is referred to as 'shining one' in Ezekiel and a description from my research project on the Bible follows in the next paragraph. This was one of the points in the project where it began to dawn on me that we all may have missed something—you will see this in my notes. The passage starts with God speaking to Ezekiel:

'Thou shalt burn with fire (217-uwr-flame, region of light [from 215-owr-to be luminous, break of day, glorious, set on fire, shine [NOTE: After noting OWR and UWR for 2/3 of this work—God grants me to stumble on this suffix and its meaning! The creatures that have this as part of their name {chamOWR, tOWR, shOWR, etc. must have some ability to emit light or discharge fire—truly impressive creatures—fire breathing dragons? God had me researching Ezekiel's word to the king of Tyrus (a synonym for satan) when He had me see this aberration in word choice for fire. In probably 400 uses in the OT, this word for fire is used only a handful of times.])'

'Afterward he brought me to the gate; the gate that looketh toward the east and behold!—the glory of the God of Israel came from the way of the east. And His Voice!—like a noise of many waters—and the earth shined (215-owr-to be luminous [NOTE: A root word; this use describing the glory of God gives us a good indication that the critters with this as part of their name had a similar characteristic! English-ass; Hebrew-chamOWR. In English; a dull brown or grey critter—In Hebrew; something that shares the glorious shine of God?! There IS a disconnect here!!!]) . . . '

As you can see; I believe there is more research needing to be done—I do not know what to make of this disconnect; but someone more learned in Hebrew might be able to figure it out. It may come down to a jot or tittle in the Hebrew—things I do not know about right now.

There are also questions raised when the environments a critter is said to live in does not match the English animal or a characteristic of an animal. These English language inconsistencies argue against the critter's English identity. Another inconsistency occurs when lengthy lists of critters appear where the English identity of the critters does not make much sense. Since the Bible is inerrant IN ITS ORIGINAL LANGUAGE as understood by its ORIGINAL AUDIENCE; these inconsistencies will one day be understood and made clear—even if that day is in Heaven.

However; make no mistake here ye servants of satan who will seek to distort what I am saying because your master knows that his rule over men's minds regarding dinosaurs is about to end: God's Word is perfect!—and He overrode the human fallibility of the ones He chose as His authors WHEN they were writing what would become Scripture. The translators in 1611 were NOT inspired **authors** of Scripture—only translating and transliterating from the original to a new language. They did the best they could with what they knew and believed at the time—some gave their lives in defiance of a tyrant who would have had NO translation into an understandable language of the ordinary people occur. I do not fault the translators from their day—I make no claim that I have it all right in this work and I make that plain in the body of this work. Let us move on.

So when inconsistency of list conflicts with the critter's identity—or when characteristics of animals do not match—or when environmental setting mismatch occurs: We have valid reason to look more closely and request more expert people to figure out the issue. There are many such examples that I cite in my Research Project of the entire Bible (scholars who desire to do more research may request a copy to save you time; if you have valid credentials I will give you one for the $5 cost of production and postage)—a sampling of them follows on the next page:

Inconsistency of List Examples:

From Leviticus 11: [All in this list are supposed to be creatures with wings, but are not necessarily birds]

"And these ye shall have in abomination among the fowls (5775-owph), they shall not be eaten, they an abomination:

the eagle (5404-[exclusively as eagle OT, twice conjuncted with gier]nesher-to lacerate),
and the ossifrage (6538-[used twice OT] perec-{from 6536-parac-break in pieces} claw),
and the ospray (5822-[used twice OT] ozniyah-{probably from 5797-'oz-[from 5810-azaz-be stout, harden, prevail]boldness, might, power}strength),
and the vulture (1676-[used once, different in Deuteronomy] da'ah-{from 1675-da'ah-dart, fly rapidly}the kite from rapid flight),

and the kite (344-[twice in OT] ayah-screamer), after his
kind, every raven (6158-[exclusive OT] oreb/
owreb-{from 6150-arab-[like 6148 in idea covering
with texture] grow dusky, be darkened}dusky
hue) after his kind (NOTE: pre-fix OWR in one
rendering)

and the owl (1328,3284-[here&Deuteronomy and plural
only compounded this way, other words translated
singular owl; Lev&Deut 3563 & 3244, Psalm 102
3563, Isaiah 3244,3917,7091] bethuel & ya'anah—
destroyer of God, a place in Palestine & feminine
of 3283-answering cry),

and the night hawk (8464-[same in Deuteronomy for
night hawk] tachmac—from its violence, owl,
nighthawk),

and the cuckow (7828-[same in Deuteronomy] shachaph—
peel, emaciate, gull),

and the hawk (5322-[same in Deuteronomy&Job] brilliance,
flashing speed), after his kind,

and the little owl (3563-kowc-hold together, cup/cuplike
as container),

and the cormorant (7994-[here and Deuteronomy, 6893
in Isa&Zeph] shalak{from 7993-shalak-throw out,
adventure, cast away/cast forth, hurl}casting as into
the sea),

and the great owl (3244-[from 5398-nashaph-breeze, blow
like the wind]from its blowing cry),

and the swan (8580-[used here and Deuteronomy]
tanshemeth-{from 5395-nasham-blow away,
destroy}NOTE: root 8565-tan-elongate, monster;
a sea serpent/other huge marine animal: ALSO
tan is root to 8577-TANNIYN-dragon, serpent,
whale!),

and the pelican (6893-[used 3 times; here, Deuteronomy/
Psalm 102] qa'ath-{from 6958-qow/qayah-vomit}
vomiting),

and the gier eagle (7360-racham/rachamah-{from 7355-to
fondle, love}vulture, tender towards young),

and the stork (2624-[used 5 times OT] chaciydah-feminine of 2623, maternal, kind), the heron (601-[used here/ Deuteronomy only] 'anaphah-{from 599-anaph-breath hard in enraged/angry way}irascible, perhaps parrot) after her kind,

and the lapwing (1744-[used here and Deuteronomy] duwkiyphath-uncertain, hoopoe/ grouse), and the bat (5847-[used here and Deuteronomy] atalleph-uncertain, a bat).

All fowls (5775-owph) that creep (8318-sherets), going upon four [NOTE: Implies aforementioned list has wings/four feet or hooves, birds? NO! Types of winged lizards/dragons? Matches!], an abomination unto you.

From Psalm 148: **'Praise the Lord. Praise ye the Lord from the heavens; praise Him in the heights. Praise ye Him all His angels; praise ye Him all His hosts. Praise ye Him sun and moon. Praise Him all ye stars of light. Praise Him, ye heavens of heavens and ye waters that above the heavens. Let them praise the Name of the Lord; for He commanded and they were created. He hath also stablished them for ever and ever; He hath made a decree which shall not pass. Praise the Lord from the earth ye dragons** (8577-tanniyn) **and all deeps. Fire and hail; snow and vapours; stormy wind fulfilling His Word; mountains and all hills; fruitful trees and all cedars; beasts** (2416-chay) **and all cattle** (930-behemoth)**; creeping** (7431-remes-reptiles) **things and flying** (3671-kanaph-an edge or extremity [from 3670-kanaph-to project laterally]) **fowl** (6833-tsippowr NOTE: Look at this impressive list of the greatest creatures and forces known to man—the last item: Tsippowr—if understood in its conventional sense: A little hopping bird—DOESN'T FIT the pattern! Of the animals specifically called out {exclude beasts which is chay, the general term of a living thing} mentioned—dragons, behemoth, remes=reptiles, little hopping birds??? No way!—this has to be an incorrect rendering. As I have pointed out earlier, tsippOWR has the characteristic ending of several other critters I think are dinosaurs: chamOWR {asses}, tOWR and shOWR, etc.). **Kings of the earth and all people; princes and all judges of the earth. Both young men and maidens; old men and children.**

**Let them praise the Name of the Lord; for His Name alone
is excellent; His glory—above the earth and heaven! He also
exalteth the horn of His people; the praise of all His saints of
the children of Israel; a people near unto Him. Praise ye the
Lord!'**

A further note: This Psalm was most likely written by king
Hezekiah. In another section of Scripture—it is said that he kept many
behema as pets or zoo creatures. Would his great collection include a
common 'little hopping bird' that would be found commonly?—I think
not. TsippOWR is a creature we need to look into much more.

Inconsistency of Anatomical Characteristic Examples:

Psalm 68: **'The Lord gave the word; great the company of
those that published. Kings of armies did flee apace and she
that tarried at home divided the spoil. Though ye have lien
among the pots; the wings** (3671-kanaph-edge, extremity) **of a
dove** (3123—yownah) **covered with silver** (keceph-pale color-most
often refers to actual silver or other money; doubtful that a literal
meaning intended here, but rather this is the color of yownah's wings)
and her feathers (84-ebrah-feather or wing-feminine of 83-pinion
or long wing) **with yellow** (3422-yeraqraq-greenish yellow-{from
3418-yaraq-vacuity of color, pallor, yellow-green of young or sickly
vegetation[from 3417-yaraq-to spit]}) **gold** (2742-charuwts-incised,
gold-as mined, a threshing sledge having sharp teeth{pass part of
2782-charats-to point sharply, to wound}NOTE: Once again, when
the Hebrew is fleshed out, the creature described bears little resemblance
to the English creature named a dove. Since when do doves have a pallor
color, greenish-yellow on their long wing with sharp points on the
wing? This more properly fits a dragon or pterodactyl! Why call it a
dove?—and yet this is the same creature Noah let loose that went out
and TORE A BRANCH OFF of a tree and when it returned, had to
be hauled into the ark—this DOES NOT sound like any dove I have
ever seen!!) **when the Almighty scattered kings in it; it was as
snow in Salmon. The hill of God; the hill of Bashan—an high
hill; the hill of Bashan. Why leap ye, ye high hills? The hill
God desireth to dwell in; yea, the Lord will dwell for ever. The**

chariots of God; twenty thousand, thousands of angels; the Lord among them; Sinai, in the holy place. Thou hast ascended on high; thou hast led captivity captive. Yea, the rebellious also, that the Lord God might dwell. Blessed the Lord; daily leadeth us, the God of our salvation.' Selah.

From the book of Daniel; King Nebuchadnezzar's second dream: "Thus; the visions of mine head in my bed. I saw—and behold!—a tree in the midst of the earth!—and the height thereof: Great! The tree grew and was strong and the height thereof reached unto heaven—and the sight thereof: To the end of all the earth!—The leaves thereof: Fair!—and the fruit thereof: Much!—and in it: Meat for all. The beasts (2423) of the field had shadow under it and the fowls (6853-tsephar-bird {Chaldean corresponding to Hebrew 6833—tsippowr} NOTE: Recall that the ONLY description of a tsippOWR could not be some little bird but more likely fits a flying reptile. NOTE: Just found 5783&4 UWR meaning naked or bare or chaff and 5785-OWR meaning skin, naked, hide or leather—obviously someone better versed in Hebrew is needed to sort this out!!!) of the heaven dwelt in the boughs thereof and all flesh was fed of it.

"This: The interpretation O king and this: The decree of the most High—which is come upon my lord the king: That they shall drive thee from men and thy dwelling shall be with the beasts (2423) of the field and they shall make thee to eat grass as oxen (8450-tOWR-bull {Chaldean corresponds to Hebrew 7794-shOWR}) and they shall wet thee with the dew of heaven—and seven times shall pass over thee: Till thou know that the Most High ruleth in the kingdom of men and giveth it to whomsoever He will—and whereas they commanded to leave the stump of the tree roots: Thy kingdom shall be sure unto thee—after that thou shalt have known that the heavens do rule. Wherefore, O king! Let my counsel be acceptable unto thee and break off thy sins by righteousness and thine iniquities by shewing mercy to the poor—if it may be a lengthening of thy tranquility."

'All this came upon the king Nebuchadnezzar. At the end of twelve months; he walked in the palace of the kingdom of

Babylon. The king spake and said, "Is not this great Babylon that I have built for the house of the kingdom by the might of my power and for the honour of my majesty?" While the word in the king's mouth: There fell a voice from heaven, "O king Nebuchadnezzar! To thee it is spoken: The kingdom is departed from thee!—and they shall drive thee from men—and thy dwelling: With the beasts (2423) of the field! They shall make thee to eat grass as oxen (8450)!—and seven times shall pass over thee until thou know that the most High ruleth in the kingdom of men—and giveth it to whomsoever He will." The same hour was the thing fulfilled upon Nebuchadnezzar!— and he was driven from men and did eat grass as oxen (8450) and his body was wet with the dew of heaven till his hairs (8177-sear {Chaldean corresponding to Hebrew 8181-sear-disheveled, tossed or bristling [from 8175-saar-to storm, be horribly afraid]}) **were grown like eagle's** (5403-neshar {Chaldean corresponding to Hebrew 5404-nesher-to lacerate}) **and his nails** (2953-tephar-fingernail, hoof or claw {Chaldean means the same as Hebrew 6856-tsipporen-sense from 6833 meaning scratching}claw, human nail, point of a style or pen) **like a bird's** (6853-tsephar! {NOTE: Here is the Chaldean equivalent to 6833-tsippowr. This description is applied to a full grown man while 6833 says "little hopping bird"—SOMETHING is amiss here! My suspicion is that 6833 is a much larger, potentially dragon-like critter. Why would a little hopping bird be likened to the greatest king of that era and especially be said to have claws akin to a 5404-nesher-lacerator? We need a complete re-look at the Hebrew language by EXPERTS who will take the questions I raise seriously instead of simply believing those that taught them a particular view! All I can do is raise questions and notice patterns!}) . . . ."'".

Inconsistency of Environmental Setting Examples:

Psalm 102: 'Hear my prayer, O Lord, and let my cry come unto Thee. Hide not Thy face from me in the day I am in trouble; incline Thine ear unto me in the day I call, answer me speedily. For my days are consumed like smoke and my bones are burned as an hearth. My heart is smitten and withered like grass so that I forget to eat my bread. By reason of the voice of

my groaning my bones cleave to my skin. I am like a pelican (6893 NOTE: Hebrew word simply means vomiting; apparently this creature regurgitates its food; there is NO implication of what that food is; i.e. fish, a pelican's normal food or of how or where that food is caught) **of the wilderness** (4057-midbar-NOTE: This is the same Hebrew word for the Sinai wanderings; i.e. DESERT/DRY where God through Moses had to perform miracles to get ANY WATER—what on earth would a pelican be doing there {except dying}? This creature CANNOT be a pelican!)**; I am like an owl** (3563 NOTE: Same words as used for pelican and little owl in Lev 11 and Deut 14 in the lists of clean / unclean creatures. As I argue there, this list may well be of flying reptiles rather than birds) **of the desert."**

From Ezekiel 7: **"Behold! The day! Behold! It is come! The morning is gone forth! The rod hath blossomed; pride that budded. Violence is risen up into a rod of wickedness. None of them—nor of their multitude—nor any of their's; neither wailing for them. The time is come; the day draweth near—let not the buyer rejoice nor the seller mourn—for wrath upon all the multitude thereof. For the seller shall not return to that which is sold; although they were yet alive—for the vision!— touching the whole multitude thereof shall not return—neither shall any strengthen himself in the iniquity of his life. They have blown the trumpet; even to make all ready—but none goeth to the battle; for My wrath—upon all the multitude thereof. The sword; without—and the pestilence and the famine within. He that in the field shall die with the sword and he that in the city—famine and pestilence shall devour him. But they that escape of them shall escape and shall be on the mountains like doves** (3123) **of the valleys** (1516-gay-lofty sides, gorge NOTE: Not the usual habitat of what we would think of as a dove. A pterodactyl, sure. Dove, nah.)**—all of them mourning** (1993-hamah-make a loud sound, be in great commotion or tumult, to rage, war, moan, clamour, be in an uproar, roar NOTE: This CANNOT be a dove as we know it! There are appropriate Hebrew words for the sound that even an agitated English dove would make—these are not used. This critter, the yownah, could not have been the English dove! A pterodactyl? From legends it lives in the cited environment and is purported to make the sound identified here!)**; every one for his iniquity."**

Here are the animals that share the OWR prefix or suffix or in the middle of the critter's Hebrew name—often the word in English is not always transliterated the same. Where that occurs I will do my best to tell you:

1) Cham**owr** (word 2543)—one of five Hebrew words transliterated as: Ass / Asses. Of the 78 times Ass / Asses appears in English—56 times it is the word Chamowr. In those contexts it is clearly a beast of burden. Its name only means 'dun red'. It is the animal in Leviticus whose neck is to be broken if its firstborn is not redeemed to God. As such; it is under the sub-heading of behema—large quadrupeds. The English ass is not in the same size class as an elephant or Brachiosaurus.

2) Sh**owr** (word 7794)—one of nine Hebrew words transliterated as: Ox / Oxen. Of the 139 times Ox / Oxen appears in English—61 times it is the word Showr. The word baqar—which is more likely the English Ox and is the animal Solomon made images of—appears 66 times. Solomon was not punished for making graven images of baqar and was the wisest man ever—I figure his word is our word ox. The Showr means 'a traveler'.

3) T**owr**—(word 8449 transliterated as turtledove)

4) Tsipp**owr**—(word 6833)—one of four Hebrew words transliterated as: Bird / Bird's / Birds. Of the 44 times Bird / Bird's / Birds appears in English—31 times it is word Tsippowr. Eight other times the word Owph is used; meaning something with wings/feathers. I find it odd that NONE of the contexts in which this word is found DEMANDS that the critter be a bird and many contexts do not even require the critter to have wings! The word for fowler simply means to ensnare. In 1611 men used birds to hunt and trapped birds with snares—but this does not mean the ancient Hebrews did! There is also a quote; **'I will give thee unto the ravenous** (5861-ayit) **birds** (6833-tsippowr . . . NOTE: Wait just a minute! Up until now tsippowr has been used for a sparrow or other small hopping bird. Are sparrows to be converted to

ravenous carnivores? Once again something has been lost in the translation to English—the suffix OWR as recently discovered means {217-uwr-flame, region of light [from 215-owr-to be luminous, break of day, glorious, set on fire, shine—or bare, naked hide} This CANNOT be a sparrow or other small hopping bird! This MUST BE something else!) **of every sort and the beasts** (2416) **of the field to be devoured.'**

5) Gibb**owr**—word 1368—translated mighty; means powerful, warrior, tyrant, champion, giant. NOTE: Many contexts—if one takes this word to mean a type of dinosaur; the many 'mighty men of valour' phrases could mean those who fight in war mounted on dinosaurs. King Saul's father Kish may have raised fighting dinosaurs; for he was **'a mighty** (gibbowr) **man of power** (chayil-derived from word meaning to twist, writhe or whirl).**'** Not all contexts fit this interpretation—but many could.) Gibbowr occurs 133 times of the approximately 245 times mighty is used. At least 13 Hebrew words translate into English as 'mighty'.

6) **Owr**eb—word 6158—meaning 'dusky hue'; transliterated as raven all ten times it appears. What the creature actually is we do not know. None of the contexts demand that it even be a bird or have wings (it is sent out with the dove by Noah; but as we have seen, Yownah—the dove, may not have been a dove, either!).

7) Bek**owr**-1060-firstborn & thus chief

8) Deb**owr**ah-1682-bees-orderly motion or systematic instincts; bee

9) Der**owr**-1866-the swallow-applied to a bird; a swift or some type of swallow-same as 1865-move rapidly, freedom, spontaneity

10) ★G**owr**-5286-naar-to growl **'they shall yell** (5286) **as lion's** (738) **whelps** (1484).**'**

11) ★Ch**owr**-2356-cavity, cave, den [NOTE: The size of the dwelling of the "asp" is apparently larger than for just a

snake. Add to this the "OWR" suffix and we may have here another larger reptile]) the sucking child shall play on the hole of the asp (6620-pethen)

*The last two references may not be animals in and of themselves but characteristics or places they live. I included them here to be honest with my readers that there are unanswered questions about this topic—and hopefully to pique the interest of some Hebrew scholar who will take up this challenge.

Did Jesus Christ ride a dinosaur into Jerusalem on Palm Sunday? Here is the passage from the Gospel of Matthew:

[21] 'And when they drew nigh unto Jerusalem and were come to Bethphage; unto the mount of Olives—then sent Jesus two disciples saying unto them, "Go into the village over against you." and "Straightway ye shall find an ass (3688-onos-apparently a primary word-donkey [NOTE: In this prophecy fulfilling passage—it is important to ensure that Jesus rides on the correct animal! If He doesn't; He doesn't fulfill prophecy—i.e. He could not be who He claimed to be. The OT prophecy is found in Zechariah 9:9 " . . . lowly; and riding upon an ass {2543-chamowr}" My OT research clearly shows that this critter is a type of behema. The NT reference has Jesus telling his disciples to go look for a particular set of animals. The OT prophecy doesn't speak to where He would get the animals—unimportant EXCEPT that in this animal based economy there could be literally hundreds of such pairs of animals all over the land. It seems odd that THE prophecy to identify THE CHRIST would be so loose! Could there be more here? NOTICE that BOTH the English words for ass and colt are the first time they appear in the NT and BOTH are 'primary words'—translator code for 'we couldn't find a derivation so we conclude it must be a word originating in the Greek culture. The English translators are ~1600 yrs removed from the event and are confronted with a word they don't understand. They have no choice but to choose a word their audience would understand—consistent with traditions of the Church handed down to them. MY POINT: The OT chamowr—as with all domesticated large reptiles—were getting rarer through the centuries. It would have been easy to find a pair of large domesticated reptiles in a time where domesticated animals had largely shifted to mammal kinds; except for a few who clung to the 'classics' like those who drive '57 Chevy T-birds today. A Messianic impostor—of which we were told there were at least a few—would likely have misinterpreted the passages of prophecy for the mammal kind of animal—and tried to ride into Jerusalem as the Messiah. Jesus; knowing exactly WHICH type of animal to ride—and being Lord; having preserved some for this very occasion—would certainly have made headlines. The Pharisees would have scrambled to pull out the prophecy and verify the type of animal—as this would have been an easy way of showing Jesus to be an impostor; but they do not accuse Him of riding the wrong type of animal. I am only surmising here—it is likely not possible for anyone to prove it one way or another unless there is some expert in Greek and Hebrew that could do more research than Dr. Strong was able to.]) **tied and a colt** (4454-polos-apparently a primary word; filly [NOTE: Philly is simply a guess on the part of the translators—see lengthy note above on ass.]) **with her. Loose and bring unto me." and "If any say ought unto you; ye shall say, 'The Lord hath need of them' and straightway he will send them." All this was done that it might be fulfilled which was spoken by the prophet saying, "Tell ye the daughter of Sion, 'Behold!—thy King cometh unto thee; meek and sitting upon an ass** (3688-onos) **and a colt** (4454) **the foal** (5207-huios-son) **of an ass** (5268-hupozugion-animal under a yoke, draught-beast [NOTE: This word means only that this is a beast recognized as domesticated and being used for labor—it DOES NOT identify the type of animal.]).'"

So did Jesus ride a dinosaur? You; like I—will have to ask Him when we get to Heaven. That is; if you are going to Heaven. Are you going to Heaven? Do you know for sure? You can know for sure that you are going to Heaven by doing what one man did! This man was the only man in the whole New Testament that Jesus Himself told would go to Heaven: The thief on the cross next to His. This man did three things: 1) He recognized he was a sinner (. . . We; are justly punished for our crimes!)—2) He recognized Jesus was the Messiah (. . . but this man has done nothing wrong {calling Jesus righteous in the Hebrew culture equated Him with God})—3) He asked Jesus to save him (Jesus—remember me!—when You come into Your Kingdom!!). This man was hours from death and nailed to a cross—he could DO nothing to earn salvation. This man could only ask for mercy from God's Son—and accept it as a free gift if Jesus granted it.

What did Jesus say? "I tell you the truth! This day you will be with Me in paradise!" Getting saved is this simple. You have sinned; haven't you? You; being a human—cannot pay that kind of debt with anything you might get in this world. You; like me and every other human need a Savior. There is only One: Jesus. Buddha, Ghandi, Mohammad and all other 'religious' men are dead. Jesus bodily rose from the grave—skeptics have tried to prove this Doctrine wrong—and became Christians when they could not! Recognize that Jesus is the Way—the Truth—the Life—your Messiah! Now ask Him to forgive you—and be Lord of your life. Who cares what your friends think! You would likely be surprised to find out how little your friends actually do think! We are talking about eternity here—for you; not for them: Will it be smoking—or non-smoking? "Today—if you hear His voice—is the day of salvation!"—not tomorrow; not next week.

Summary of main points:

1) Much more research is needed into both the Hebrew and the Greek languages
2) There is only one Way to fellowship with God—the Lord Jesus Christ

CHAPTER TWELVE

The Ox-Bullock, Unicorn and Other Odd Critters

The fossil record shows us that there were very many types of dinosaurs. One then may legitimately ask if there are more unusual critters mentioned in Scripture. The short answer is; 'Yes!' Whether these are dinosaurs or not is not as clear as we may like, but the topic should be looked at just the same.

Let us start with the Ox-Bullock found in Psalm 69. The author of this psalm is King David and the English in the King James Bible is rendered 'ox *or* bullock'. The word 'or' is in italics just as I have shown here; which means it is a word added by the translators in 1611 to make the English make more sense. In adding that word—not found in the original text—a potential reference to a well known dinosaur: Triceratops—is largely hidden. Read the text without the 'or', " . . . than an ox-bullock that has horns and hoofs". It is the only time in the Bible that this set of words occurs together.

As previously stated; it appears to have been common practice in the Hebrew language to continue describing unique features of animals until the audience would have enough information to accurately determine what critter the writer was talking about. An example of this has already been given in Job 40:15—24 where God says, "Behold now behemoth, which I made with you, he eats grass as an ox . . . . He moves his tail like a cedar." God describes the animal until it is clear what animal He is talking about. In like fashion; King David describes enough about the animal known as the ox-bullock as ' . . . having horns and hoofs'.

I know, I know: Lots of animals have horns and hoofs. An ox has horns and hoofs; but there are other words for ox in the Hebrew language and when writers mean an ox—they select one of those words (some of which may not be ox / oxen in English—a point already covered). A bull has horns and hoofs; but the same argument can be made as for an ox. In fact; the other animals that also have horns and hoofs have specific terms in Hebrew for them as far as I can tell. Add to this the fact that the word for horns in this passage is the word used to describe ivory tusks! So the animal in question could have been an elephant if you consider its toes to be hoofs. The Hebrew word for hoofs used here is the only time it is used and means to stamp or break in pieces—again, that could be said of either an elephant or Triceratops. The ox-bullock apparently was a rare or valuable animal, because it is considered an appropriate gift to give to one's Lord. Elephants are indeed not common animals but then again; neither is a Triceratops—especially by this time in history. The reference is not clear; but is interesting just the same. I will leave it up to you to decide what you believe the ox-bullock was.

A song by the group The Irish Rovers from the 1970s was about the supposed extinction of the animal known to us as a unicorn at the time of Noah's great Flood. According to the song, the 'silly unicorns' were playing hide and seek when the rains came down and washed them away. Just what are these creatures? Let us consult the One Who made them for some answers!

The unicorn is (unicorns are) actually mentioned in the Bible nine times. It is word (7214)—reem or reeym in Hebrew and Strong's takes a guess at its identity as a wild bull, but the word itself means only that it is conspicuous. Its root word is 7213 which means ' . . . to rise, be lifted up . . . '. Modern day bulls do not generally rear up like a wild stallion does—at least as far as I know. Psalm 92:10 indicates it has some kind of projection (qeren—7161) protruding from it's head—but the word does not necessarily limit the number of such projections—so the legendary single horn on a horse-like creature is purely speculation. This is the same ivory-like projection for many animals discussed in this work such as the ox-bullock had.

The most interesting place unicorns are discussed is in Job by God Himself. God speaks from chapters 38 to 41 in the Book of Job. In chapter 38, God asks Job if he—a mere man—can control the greatest forces in the Universe, Solar System and the Earth. Then in chapter 39, God begins to discuss what logically would be the greatest animals He has ever made. He begins with some lesser creatures before talking about Behemoth and Leviathan, but one could argue that He would have kept to the same general theme—asking Job about His great dinosaurs.

The list of animals mentioned is, in order, in English: Lion, Raven, Wild Goat and Hinds, Wild Ass, Unicorn, Peacocks and Ostriches, Horse, Hawk, Eagle, Behemoth and finally Leviathan. Of this list, many of these animals have already been shown to NOT be the English identified animal by characteristic, description of body part or environment. The word peacock appears only twice in English—and it is two different words in Hebrew. In the context of God's discussion here—He would have kept to a consistent list: His greatest dinosaurs— not dodged around the animal kingdom the way the English does. As with the Ox-Bullock—you will have to decide what a unicorn actually was—but it seems clear that it was not a horse sporting a single horn.

Another interesting possible dinosaur is the animal identified in English as a lion (3833). That's right, a lion! The basic word translated as lion is another transliteration of a characteristic of an animal. The Hebrew word means 'roarer' and also appears in the list of God's greatest and fiercest animal creations of Job 39. A less often used Hebrew word also transliterated lion means 'mane'. Sometimes the word is further described as a young lion or old lion and other descriptions. The story of Samson killing the lion describes the honey found later in the canopied carcass—since when do lions have canopies? They have manes; but not a body structure that would be called a canopy. Once again from the Hebrew; there really is no way to accurately determine what animal is being described. All we know is that the critter roars and is a fairly commonly encountered animal. King David as a boy 'killed the lion and the bear' with his slingshot. The Hebrew rendering is that David killed the roarer and the paw. Obviously these creatures were ferocious animals; but were they the mammals we know or were they dinosaurs such as raptors? If there is a Hebrew expert out there up to the challenge; we may not have to wait to find out for sure until we get to Heaven.

Apes and peacocks are very distinct animals in English—are they in the Hebrew? A look at 1 Kings 10 gives us the answer: 'And all king Solomon's drinking vessels: Gold—and all the vessels of the house of the forest of Lebanon: Pure gold; none silver—it was nothing accounted of in the days of Solomon; for the king had at sea a navy of Tharshish with the navy of Hiram, once in three years came the navy of Tharshish bringing gold and silver; ivory and apes (6971-qowph-uncertain derivation{but note that this word is owph {thing with wings} with a q in front!? Interesting!}) and peacocks (8500-tukkiy or tuwkkiy-probably some imported creature [one other word is translated peacocks in Job 39:13 and used in conjunction with wings, this creature is not said to have wings while the qowph just prior may well have had wings]). So king Solomon exceeded all the kings of the earth for riches and for wisdom. And all the earth sought to Solomon to hear his wisdom which God had put in his heart.' Were these creatures the English identified ones? All one can do is research and draw a conclusion.

Ravens are said to have fed Elijah 'meat' while he was hiding from King Ahab after he pronounced God's punishment of devastating drought on the sinning nation of Israel. Meat in the Old Testament can mean bread, but this word indicates it can also mean food in general or even prey as in hunted lesser animals. In every picture Bible I have seen, this creature is depicted as a large crow flying in with bread in its beak.

Yet we must consider that the raven also is included in the list of Job 39 among God's other great creatures which logic suggests were probably the great dinosaurs. It should be noted that in every context of its use; ravens need not be birds or even have wings! Yet Noah dispatched the raven and the dove to see if the waters of the Flood had subsided—and we have seen that the identity of the dove (yownah) is suspect.

One more clue that throws suspicion on the English identity of the raven: In Job it is said that the raven wanders around trying to find food for its young that are crying out with hunger. The word rendered wander is (8582—ta'ah) and can be rendered into many possible English words—none of which involve flying. One would think that if the raven were actually a bird of some sort, it would be depicted in one of its nine renderings as actually doing what all birds do: Fly.

The ram is yet another odd critter in the Hebrew, while it is very definite in English. It is word (352) ayil which means strength, chief, strong support—and has a note stating that it is essentially the same in meaning as word (193)—uwl. The word uwl means: To twist, be strong (the body as being rolled together). What? An English ram is a smaller than a horse animal. It is not what the Hebrew people would consider 'chief'—and it certainly would not have a body considered to be 'rolled together'. One last appeal to you Hebrew scholars looking for a challenge! This is important, for it was a ram (ayil) that Abraham sacrificed in place of Isaac.

The saytr (8163) is the last odd creature we will take a quick look at, though there are more we could examine. Isaiah is the only one who uses the word and it means shaggy, he-goat, a faun, devil. It apparently was derived from word (8175) sa'ar—storm, shiver, be horribly afraid. This is the same description as was used when the Bible describes what happened to Nebuchanezzar with regard to the hairs of his body. In the chapter 34 context; it is found in a long list of creatures that includes the unicorn, bullocks (6499-par), bulls (47-abbiyr)—all of which are described as strong!—chief!—powerful! It would seem that the satyrs also were some type of animal similar to these, which more and more seem to be some kind of 'terrible lizard' or dinosaur. In the chapter 13 context, the satyr moves into the ruins of man's cities after war has destroyed it along with 'doleful creatures' and owls (for which no Strong's definition exists). The dragon was said to do the same thing—for there was a dragon-well outside of the ruined Jerusalem that Nehemiah rode by on his domesticated behema.

With respect to what these odd critters were; I have done my best to try to raise interest in someone greater than I with regard to ancient Hebrew and Greek to figure it out. May God grant that person or persons sufficient ability and desire to unlock the mysteries that I have but begun to probe!

Summary of main points:

1) There are many creatures mentioned in the Bible—all of which have English names, but may be dinosaurs
2) Man has always existed with dinosaurs in the historical past as recorded in the most dependable Book ever written: The Holy Bible!
3) I do not have the ability to figure them out any more than I have—and so I appeal to some Hebrew and Greek scholar somewhere to do it

CONCLUSION

This book has explored some very interesting possibilities regarding large reptiles known today from the fossil record as dinosaurs. Many; including me; wondered why there seemed to be no references to dinosaurs in the Bible. Little did I know what some research would reveal. I have no idea what impact this book will have on today's world—perhaps it will be ignored as lunatic fringe musing—but then again; I wrote it to capture the glory God deserves for being the Creator of the dinosaurs from the devil who has perverted man's understanding on this critical issue. Many reject the Bible for this very reason—they can see dinosaur skeletons in museums and read the made-up stories of evolutionists regarding them; but cannot find references to them in the English renditions of God's Book; nor are they Hebrew or Greek scholars.

Since I believe this book could have major impact and is a direct attack on satan (I refuse to capitalize his name!)—I know that he will do all he can to discredit me and/or the ideas presented herein. I will trust in the Scripture that states confidently that He Who is in the believer (God the Holy Spirit) is greater than he who is in the world (satan). May God finally recover the glory for these critters! May He grant that I get to have some pet dinosaurs in Heaven! How cool would that be!!

I will say it once again so that satan will have the most difficult time possible in discrediting this work: The Bible is God's inerrant Word! The Bible is Perfect in its Original Language as understood in its Original Culture and Era—as set down by men inspired of God—in whom God supernaturally set aside their human imperfectness for the time they were writing Scripture for Him. The translation into English IS NOT any more without inconsistencies than when the Bible is translated into any other language! God continues to provide man with more and better understanding as discoveries are made and false claims are debunked such as evolution's 'billions of years' and 'no men with dinosaurs' dogmas. When such research is done—we always find the

Bible in its original language and understood from it original culture is ALWAYS right. We must adjust our thinking to God's Word—we must NOT adjust God's Word to fit our human understanding or claims.

So be assured: Dinosaurs were created on days five and six by God and have always lived with man—some may still be alive today. The pages of Scripture do record these events as HISTORY (God's story—HIS STORY—get it?). He created the Universe (Uni—single; Verse—spoken sentence: God spoke everything into existence with a single sentence that comprises our first chapter of Genesis—in the Hebrew: It is one long sentence!).

No Christian DOCTRINES are affected or altered or even questioned by the ideas presented in this work: Man is a sinner in need of forgiveness; Jesus' work on the cross is the ONLY payment for that sin acceptable to God; God will save ONLY those who trust in Jesus! Thank you God for sending Your Son; Jesus—to die on the cross for us—and for raising Him up from the dead! This is the faith by which we are saved—what you believe about the contents of this book regarding the fantastic creatures we call dinosaurs is of much less importance. What you think or say about me—genius or lunatic—is of no consequence at all.

May God get the glory in all things! Now—including dinosaurs!!

APPENDIX I

Uses of Behemoth / Behema

The following table is derived from Strong's and details the uses of behemoth and behema—along with the book of the Bible where it is found, who used the word and my comments on the use:

Uses of Behemoth and Behema			
Word w/ English Rendering	Chapter and Verse	Who used the word	Comment on context
Behemoth—Cattle	Genesis 1:24	God	First use of Behemoth;—Commanded by God to be created
	Genesis 1:25	Moses	Result of command—behemoth created
	Genesis 1:26	God	Man given charge over behemoth
	Genesis 2:20	Moses	Adam names all types of behemoth; word used collectively
	Genesis 3:14	God	Serpent (nachash) cursed above all behemoth; was a type of behemoth!
Behema—Beast	Genesis 6:7	God	God pronounces destruction on '. . . man and beast . . .' —1st time God associates man and beast's fate together. This happens many times in the rest of the Old Testament.
Behemoth—Cattle	Genesis 6:20	God	God directing Noah to bring behemoth onto the ark
Behema—Beast	Genesis 7:2	God	God commands Noah to take clean behema on the ark by sevens—introduces idea of 'clean' and 'unclean' for first time—sets stage for Jewish Law!

Behema—Beasts	Genesis 7:2	God	God commands Noah to also take unclean behema on the ark by twos
	Genesis 7:8	Moses	Noah obeyed God in bringing behema onto the ark
Behemoth—Cattle	Genesis 7:14	Moses	Records Noah has behemoth on the ark
	Genesis 7:21	Moses	Records the flood's killing of behemoth not on the ark
	Genesis 7:23	Moses	Confirms statement above
	Genesis 8:1	Moses	God remembers the behemoth on the ark
	Genesis 8:17	God	God commands Noah to bring forth behemoth off the ark— behemoth could still be living today!
Behema—Beast	Genesis 8:20	Moses	Noah offers a clean behema as an offering!!!—not the currently believed Jewish sacrificial animals. This continues in Leviticus!
Behemoth—Cattle	Genesis 9:10	God	God blesses Noah and behemoth after the flood
Behema—Beast	Genesis 34:23	Shechem son of Hamor	Shechem had sex with Jacob's daughter Dinah; Shechem's father deals with Jacob for marriage—Shechem talks his fellows into accepting marriage with Jacob's family—proves behema can be domesticated!!
Behema—Beasts	Genesis 36:6	Moses	Esau departs; takes domesticated animals—cites difference between behema and bovine type animals: Behema IS NOT a cow!
Behemoth—Cattle	Genesis 47:18	People of Egypt	People of Egypt deal with Joseph for food during famine—already traded domestic behemoth for food
Behema—Beast	Exodus 8:17	Moses	Plague of lice on men and behema
	Exodus 8:18	Moses	Confirms the plague occurred as predicted

	Exodus 9:9	God	Announces plague of boils
	Exodus 9:10	Moses	Confirms the plague occurred as predicted
	Exodus 9:19	God	Announces plague of hail; Egyptians have men caring for domestic behema in the field! Were behema used to build the pyramids???
	Exodus 9:22	God	Commanding Moses to bring forth the plague of hail
	Exodus 9:25	Moses	Confirms the plague of hail occurred
Behema—Beasts	Exodus 11:5	God	Announces the plague of the death of the firstborn of men and behema
Behema—Beast	Exodus 11:7	God	Continues announcement of the plague of the death of the firstborn
	Exodus 12:12	God	Detailing the last plague— plague shall be on man and behema; man's greatest domestic animal and most prized possession!
Behemoth—Cattle	Exodus 12:29	Moses	Confirms plague occurred—ties the words behema and behemoth together as the same type of animal.
Behema—Beast	Exodus 13:2	God	Claims the firstborn of man and behema as His!
	Exodus 13:12	Moses	Instructing the Jews in God's claim on their firstborn
	Exodus 13:15	Moses	Gives reason for God's claim— the last plague that set them free.
	Exodus 19:13	Moses	Instructs Jews and their behema to keep off Mt. Sinai or suffer death.
Behemoth—Cattle	Exodus 20:10	God	Rules for the sabbath; neither men nor behemoth may work— 1st cite that behemoth were used for domesticated labor!

Behema—Beast	Exodus 22:10	God	Laws regarding a behema given to the care of another.
	Exodus 22:19	God	Law regarding having sex with a behema—capital punishment!
Behemoth—Cattle	Leviticus 1:2	God	Rule for offering a behemoth; used in Jewish sacrificial rites! Every 'Cattle' in Leviticus is behemoth—NOT a cow, sheep or goat as we understand the words today!
	Leviticus 5:2	God	Rule: unwitting touching of unclean critter.
Behema—Beast	Leviticus 7:21	God	Rule: touching an unclean critter then eating the Lord's offering
	Leviticus 7:25	God	Rule: eating the fat of the behema: First reference to behema as food!
	Leviticus 7:26	God	Rule: no eating of blood of a behema!
Behema—Beasts	Leviticus 11:2	God	Primary rules distinguishing which behema may be eaten! Refers only to types of behema "These are the (2416 chay—air breathing living things {beasts}) which ye shall eat among all the (929 behema {beasts}) that on the earth . . ."—there must be many types of behemoth and behema; as a word; must also be a grouping or major 'kind' having many sub-kinds of which only some were 'unclean'.
	Leviticus 11:3	God	Some behema 'chew the cud'—this is NOT a rabbit as some say.
Behema—Beast	Leviticus 11:26	God	Some behema 'divideth the hoof (parcah—can mean "a claw"!) . . . ' could this behema be a raptor?—for it does not 'chew the cud . . ." It certainly is not some bovine or rabbit.
	Leviticus 11:39	God	God says certain behema may be eaten!

Behema—Beasts	Leviticus 11:46	God	Summary statement of the Law of behema that may be eaten without imputing uncleanness to oneself
Behema—Beast	Leviticus 18:23 (two uses)	God	Forbids man/woman to "lie with a beast"—apparently this was a Canaanite practice
Behemoth—Cattle	Leviticus 19:19	God	No hybrid breeding of behemoth
Behema—Beast	Leviticus 20:15 (two uses)	God	Capital punishment for man and beast if man has sex with behema
	Leviticus 20:16 (two uses)	God	Capital punishment for woman who try the same perversion as men
Behema—Beasts and Beast in same verse	Leviticus 20:25 (beasts 1st then beast)	God	Summary statement to separate oneself from the unclean as defined by God (not as defined by men)
Behema—Beast (3 uses; 1st & last nephesh; middle behema)	Leviticus 24:18	God	If a man kills a behema; he must make it good to the owner. Apparently behema were of considerable value.
Behemoth—Cattle	Leviticus 25:7	God	Behemoth are vegetarian; God provides their food
	Leviticus 26:22	God	Curse for disobedience: Killing of behemoth—critters essential to the economy—like our semi-trucks.
Behema—Beast	Leviticus 27:9	God	Offering a behema to God is a holy and considerable offering!
	Leviticus 27:10 (two uses)	God	More detail for offering behema to God.
Behema—Beast	Leviticus 27:11 (two uses)	God	Detail for offering unclean behema to God.
Behema—Beasts	Leviticus 27:26	God	All behema firstlings are God's
Behema—Beast	Leviticus 27:27	God	Rule for unclean behema offered to God
	Leviticus 27:28	God	Behema offered to God may not be sold or redeemed; irrevocable gift

	Numbers 3:13	God	Firstborn of man and behema are God's—reminds of last plague on Egypt as basis
Behemoth—Cattle	Numbers 3:41 (two uses)	God	God changes His claim to the firstborn of the Levites (behemoth and men).
	Numbers 3:45	God	Command to Moses to take firstborn behemoth and Levite
Behema—Beast	Numbers 8:17	God	God now uses behema instead of behemoth in claim on firstborn—must be the same 'kind' of animal!
Behema—Beasts	Numbers 18:15 (two uses)	God	Yet another claim on the firstborn of men and behema
Behemoth—Cattle	Numbers 31:9	Moses	Behemoth taken as spoils of war with the Midianites
Behema—Beasts	Numbers 31:11	Moses	Now it is behema taken as spoils of the Midianite battle— more evidence that behema / behemoth are same 'kind' creatures—separate from other animals captured
Behema—Beast	Numbers 31:26	God	God divides the spoils of war in men and behema
Behema—Beasts	Numbers 31:30	God	More detail on dividing spoils: God differentiates between types of animals! Makes clear that behema are not 'beeves'—i.e. cows or bulls as we understand the word today!
Behema—Beast	Numbers 31:47	Moses	Details on actual division of spoils
Behemoth—Cattle	Numbers 32:26	Children of Gad/ Reuben	Request Moses leave them in Gilead—a land for behemoth
	Numbers 35:3	God	Providing cities and pastures for the Levites and their behemoth
Behemoth—Cattle	Deuteronomy 2:35	Moses	Account of defeat of Sihon and taking behemoth as war spoils— many peoples had domesticated behemoth!
	Deuteronomy 3:7	Moses	Account of defeat of Og and taking behemoth as war spoils

Behema—Beast	Deuteronomy 4:17	Moses	Prohibits making images of behema
Behemoth—Cattle	Deuteronomy 5:14	Moses	Sabbath day prohibition against man or behemoth working
	Deuteronomy 7:14	Moses	Announcing blessing of fertility on man and behemoth for obedience
	Deuteronomy 11:15	God	Announcing blessing of provision on behemoth of men for obedience
	Deuteronomy 13:15	God	Orders to utterly destroy rebellious cities: men and their behemoth—behemoth can be singular or plural!
Behema—Beasts	Deuteronomy 14:4	God	Behema that may be eaten; mirrors Leviticus 11—lists BEHEMA that may be eaten—implies all other creatures are clean / may be eaten—only certain behema are unclean—i.e. meat from today's pigs—pork—is NOT unclean!! Jewish Law refers to Behema/Behemoth!!
Behema—Beast and Beasts	Deuteronomy 14:6 (two uses)	God	Clean and unclean rules apply ONLY to certain types of behema!
Behemoth—Cattle	Deuteronomy 20:14	Moses	War in Canaan; taking spoils of women / children / behemoth
Behema—Beast	Deuteronomy 27:21	Moses	Commands the tribes to pronounce blessing / curses—one curse on men who have ritual sex with behema
Behemoth—Cattle	Deuteronomy 28:4	Moses	Blessings of fertility for behemoth for obedience to God
	Deuteronomy 28:11	Moses	Again declares God will bless by increasing behemoth for obedience
Behema—Beasts	Deuteronomy 28:26	Moses	Curses for disobedience to God: Some type of behema shall eat their dead bodies! First reference to any type of behema that is a carnivore!

Behemoth—Cattle	Deuteronomy 28:51	Moses	Curses for disobedience to God: Enemies shall take their behemoth and the result of their labor
	Deuteronomy 30:9	Moses	When the Jews repent; God will bless again they and their behemoth—obviously behemoth were integral to the Jewish nation's culture
Behema—Beasts	Deuteronomy 32:24	God	Moses' song: God's curses for disobedience; one is sending the teeth (shen-sharp; ivory; forefront) of behema on them—rules out elephants as candidate for behema; unless elephants eat meat.

End of the Pentateuch—56 phrases spoken by God; 32 phrases spoken by Moses and 3 times other people use behema / behemoth with some phrases using the words multiple times for a total of 105 uses. Clearly behema and behemoth are NOT bovine animals; are used for labor and meat; in other cultures are used for ritual sex; are prized possessions taken in war—but most of all: WELL KNOWN and essentially integrated into Jewish and all other cultures from Egypt to Canaan! No wonder God tells Job to "Behold now behemoth . . ." with full expectation that Job knows exactly what he is talking about!

Behemoth—Cattle	Joshua 8:2	God	Instructs taking spoils from Ai—behemoth of Ai may be taken
	Joshua 8:27	Author of the Book of Joshua	Records that behemoth were taken as spoils from Ai
	Joshua 11:14	Author of the Book of Joshua	Records that behemoth were taken as spoils from all the Canaanite cities conquered
	Joshua 21:2	Author of the Book of Joshua	Levites ask for cities and pastures for them and their behemoth of Joshua
Behema—Beast	Judges 20:48	Author of the Book of Judges	Extermination of Benjamin for harboring rapists/murderers according to Mosaic Law—including their behema
Behema—Beasts	I Kings 4:33	Author of Kings	Solomon "spake also of beasts . . ." behema! The wisest man ever—spoke of things he SAW!

	I Kings 18:5	King Ahab	Orders his servant to find grass during Elijah's drought to save some of the behema. Horses (cuwc) and mules (pered) are types of behema. Description of cuwc in OT is of a dragon-like critter not a horse.
Behemoth—Cattle	II Kings 3:9	Author of Kings	Military expedition against Moab; no water for behemoth with the kings—Behemoth brought for: Food for the army or a fighting platform—or BOTH!
Behema—Beasts	II Kings 3:17	God (via Elisha)	God will miraculously provide water for the men and behema
Behemoth—Cattle	I Chronicles 5:21	Author of Chronicles	Account of spoils of war against the Hagarites—behemoth taken
	I Chronicles 7:21	Author of Chronicles	Unsuccessful raid on a Canaanite town—attempted to take behemoth
	II Chronicles 14:15	Author of Chronicles	King Asa's military conquest—destroyed the 'tents (ohel-dwelling)' of the enemy behemoth—man built dwellings/likely large pens for their behemoth; expected for any DOMESTICATED critter
	II Chronicles 26:10	Author of Chronicles	King Uzziah digged many wells for his 'much behemoth'
Behema—Beasts	II Chronicles 32:28	Author of Chronicles	King Hezekiah built "stalls for all manner of behema"—there must have been many kinds of behema
Behema—Beasts	Ezra 1:4	King Cyrus	Proclamation: Provisions; including behema; were to be provided to Jews returning to Jerusalem
	Ezra 1:6	King Cyrus	Same proclamation as above— real gold, real provision and real behema to be given those returning
Behema—Beast	Nehemiah 2:12 (two uses)	Nehemiah	Nehemiah rides a behema!

	Nehemiah 2:14	Nehemiah	This animal is so large it won't fit through a gate of Jerusalem—I've seen the gate; an elephant would fit—adult Brachiosaurus would not
Behemoth—Cattle	Nehemiah 9:37	Nehemiah	During a confession prayer: Recounts why enemies have rule over them and their behemoth
	Nehemiah 10:36	Nehemiah	Recounts his efforts at religious reform—that once again offerings (including behemoth) were brought
Behema—Beasts	Job 12:7	Job	Answering Zophar's oratory
	Job 18:3	Bildad	Answering Job's oratory
	Job 35:11	Elihu	Answering Job's oratory
Behemoth—Behemoth (only time)	Job 40:15	God	God directs Job to consider behemoth; his greatest land creature—analysis of description in text
Behema—Beasts	Psalm 8:7	King David	Recalling God put all creatures under man's dominion
Behema—Beast	Psalm 36:6	King David	Pondering God's greatness; recalls the God preserves man and behema
Behema—Beasts	Psalm 49:12	King David	Man perishes; just as behema does; God's second greatest creation
	Psalm 49:20	King David	Though man is certainly God's prize creation; still perishes like behema
Behemoth—Cattle	Psalm 50:10	God via Asaph	God: All creatures his; including the 'behemoth upon a thousand hills'—must have been many behemoth!—not all in a swamp
Behema—Beast	Psalm 73:22	Likely Asaph or a priest	Writer despondent how the wicked prosper—until thinks on God's eternal justice; compares self to an ignorant behema
Behemoth—Cattle	Psalm 104:14	Unknown	Identifies grass as the food of behemoth—consistent with Job
	Psalm 107:38	Unknown	The blessing of God maintains population of behemoth

Behema—Beast	Psalm 135:8	Unknown	Writer recalls final plague in Egypt
	Psalm 147:9	Unknown	God gives food to the behema
Behemoth—Cattle	Psalm 148:10	Unknown	Praises God for creation: Angels; stars&planets–great critters: Dragons, behemoth, creeping things & flying fowl—seems dinosaurs always get man's awe
Behema—Beast	Proverbs 12:10	Solomon	Stated in Kings; Solomon spake of behema!—here says a righteous man takes care of his behema!
Behema—Beasts	Proverbs 30:30	Agur	Lion is a behema—some English identified creatures cannot be that creature! This does not mean an error in Scripture!—only man's ability to translate—in the original language: God's word is Perfect!—temporary misunderstanding DOES NOT affect ANY doctrines—EXCEPT the doctrine of evolution that man never lived w/ dinosaurs!
Behema—Beasts	Ecclesiastes 3:18	Solomon	Compares man to the behema in understanding before God
	Ecclesiastes 3:19	Solomon	Notes that man dies just as the behema die
Behema—Beast	Ecclesiastes 3:19	Solomon	Same as above—Solomon spake of behema; just as claimed in Kings
	Ecclesiastes 3:21	Solomon	Ponders if the spirit of behema goes to heaven like man's; these must indeed be awesome creatures
Behema—Beasts	Isaiah 18:6 (two uses)	God via Isaiah	Prophecy that the behema will feast on unburied war dead
	Isaiah 30:6	God via Isaiah	Behema of the south: In English—rather odd collection of critters; in Hebrew—all are or could be dinosaurs—much more consistent!
Behemoth—Cattle	Isaiah 46:1	God via Isaiah	Loads are carried by behemoth!—proof of domestication and use!

Behema—Beast	Isaiah 63:14	Isaiah	Prophecy of Christ—states behema go down to the valley; must not always live in swamps!
	Jeremiah 7:20	God via Jeremiah	God will pour out His anger on man and behema—similar to the Flood
Behema—Beasts	Jeremiah 7:33	God via Jeremiah	Unburied dead will be eaten by behema
Behema—Beast	Jeremiah 9:10	Jeremiah	Lamenting for the behema have fled
Behema—Beasts	Jeremiah 12:4	Jeremiah	Asks God how long the behema will be gone from the land
	Jeremiah 15:3	God via Jeremiah	Pronouncing severe judgment including behema eating men
	Jeremiah 16:4	God via Jeremiah	Continues judgment description; dead unburied—eaten by behema
Behema—Beasts	Jeremiah 19:7	God	Again—unburied bodies of men will be consumed by behema
Behema—Beast	Jeremiah 21:6	God	To King Zedekiah—God promises death to man and behema
	Jeremiah 27:5	God	God made man and behema—does to them to whatever he sees fit to do
	Jeremiah 31:27	God	After this judgment—God will bring again both man and behema!
	Jeremiah 32:43	God	God will cause economic recovery in the land void of man and behema
	Jeremiah 33:10 (two uses)	God	Same as above—it could well be that behema survive to this day!
	Jeremiah 33:12	God	Economic recovery will include behema
Behema—Beasts	Jeremiah 34:20	God	Final warning to King Zedekiah—dead men will be eaten by behema
Behema—Beast	Jeremiah 36:29	God	Confirms final judgment to King Zedekiah—man & behema will die

	Jeremiah 50:3	God	Prophecy against Babylon—men & behema in her will be killed; all nations apparently have domesticated behema!
	Jeremiah 51:62	Jeremiah	Instructs Seraiah what to say: Man and behema are to be cut off from Babylon
Behema—Beasts	Ezekiel 8:10	Ezekiel	Vision of Israel's elders: Have made forbidden images of abominable behema
Behema—Beast	Ezekiel 14:13	God	Declares judgment will include both man and behema
	Ezekiel 14:17	God	Continues with same judgment
	Ezekiel 14:19	God	Continues with same judgment
Behema—Beast	Ezekiel 14:21	God via Ezekiel	Continues with same judgment
	Ezekiel 25:13	God via Ezekiel	God pronounces judgment on Edom; both man and behema
	Ezekiel 29:8	God via Ezekiel	God pronounces judgment on Egypt; both man and behema
	Ezekiel 29:11	God via Ezekiel	Judgment on Egypt: Man and behema will not pass through— the two's fate linked many times
Behema—Beasts	Ezekiel 32:13	God via Ezekiel	Judgment on Babylon: Man and behema to be destroyed
Behema—Beast	Ezekiel 36:11	God via Ezekiel	God will restore both man and behema to Israel's mountains
	Ezekiel 44:31	God via Ezekiel	Restores the priest's code: Cannot eat of dead of itself or torn behema: People eat these critters!!
Behema—Beasts	Joel 1:18	Joel	Domestic behema groan in suffering brought by man's evil
	Joel 1:20	Joel	Wild behema suffer—some behema have escaped to the wilds or non-domestic behema exists
	Joel 2:22	Joel	Joel tells the behema 'relief comes'—again concern for behema!

Behema—Beast	Jonah 3:7	King of Nineveh	Proclamation that man and behema are to fast both food and water!
	Jonah 3:8	King of Nineveh	Continues that man and behema are to be covered in sackcloth!
Behemoth—Cattle	Jonah 4:11	God	God's evident concern for man & his greatest animal creation!
Behema—Beasts	Micah 5:8	God via Micah	Prophecy: The word lion (738-ariy) with behema
Behema—Beasts	Habakkuk 2:17	Habakkuk	Pronouncing and prophesying judgment including behema
Behema—Beast	Zephaniah 1:3	God	Judgment against Judah to include man and behema
Behemoth—Cattle	Haggai 1:11	God	Returned exiles were not repairing God's house; but building their own houses—God chastens man and behemoth
(Last use of Cattle for Behemoth)	Zechariah 2:4	Angel	Told by another angel: Tell Zechariah that the towns of Israel will once again have men and behemoth
(Last use of Beast for Behema)	Zechariah 8:10	God	Promises economic recovery—work for man and behema—these critters could be trained to do work!
Behema—Beasts (Last use of Beasts for Behema)	Zechariah 14:15	Zechariah	Prophesying defeat on the enemies of God including behema

The Old Testament uses of Behema and Behemoth have ended: 20 more uses of Behemoth and 70 more uses of Behema have occurred AFTER the close of the Pentateuch—clearly behemoth and behema are: Domesticated and trainable, critical to a successful economy and next in line below man as special to God. About 4000 years of history have passed—God's view of these creatures has not changed; historical writers record consistent accounts and the world's most credible and reliable sources write the accounts! It is time for God to get the credit for His creation—including dinosaurs!

Ninety-Five Theses: Evolution is a Lie!—this section of this book is adapted from the Internet Public Domain

In as much as evolution and its supporting concepts of cosmology such as 'The Big Bang' and many others **are completely wrong**—and demonstrably so—being only fallible, man-inspired interpretations of the available evidence: These 95 theses are scientific and well-reasoned points that positively refute the very premise of molecules-to-man Evolution.

What then is 'Evolution'—with a capital 'E'? *It is* **NOT** *science* and **IS** nothing less than *a full-fledged religion*; a concept that can only be believed; even though its claims fly in the face of these 95 true facts / logical arguments as well as simple common sense. Otherwise intelligent persons embrace this belief system uncritically.

Evolution and Creation can be likened to inflated balloons—ANY SINGLE argument that is valid against either is all it takes to destroy the idea. If any one of these arguments is true—Evolution is FALSE. I challenge the Evolutionists to provide ANY single valid argument proving Creation to be false. They have been trying for thousands of years and have yet to do any more than tell us they disbelieve and dislike Creation thought and its adherents.

The 95 Theses Proving Evolution is a Lie are contained on the following pages:

Laws of Nature:

1. **Conservation of Energy**: Energy can neither be created nor destroyed, only altered in form (by man). Energy exists and thus was not created by man—logically: The energy must have come from Someone or somewhere. Creation says the Creator is the source (agrees with the Law) while Evolution's Big Bang says nothing gave rise to everything including all the energy in the universe (violates the Law) {See article in National Geographic Oct 1999}.

2. **Conservation of Mass**: Mass can neither be created nor destroyed (by man). Mass exists and thus was not created by man—logically: The mass must have come from Someone or somewhere. Creation says the Creator is the source (agrees with the Law) while Evolution's Big Bang says nothing gave rise to everything including all the mass in the universe (violates the Law){Same article National Geographic Oct 1999}.

3. **Law of Motion**: In frictionless open space; with nothing to push or pull on: Objects cannot start or stop spinning by themselves. If something is spinning—some original force logically had to have begun the spinning. If ORDERLY spinning is observed as it is observed throughout the universe—logically; some original purposeful and intelligent Entity must have begun ALL this motion. Evolutionists say all this synchronized motion is only 'apparently purposeful'—why should we believe them rather than what simple logic tells us?—a Creator with a purpose established all this incredible order that we observe!

4. **Conservation of Angular Momentum**: Specific behavioral Laws govern the orbits and rotation of the planets. If the Big Bang did occur—ALL the planets in our solar system would rotate on their axis in the same direction: **They do not** (Evolution's Big Bang violates the Law). Venus rotates backward compared to Earth and Uranus rotates at a ninety degree angle with respect to

Earth. The Creator could choose to spin the planets any way desired (agrees with this Law).

5. **Law of Gravity**: Structures observed in space; such as galaxies: Mathematically could not have held together in such an ordered state for more than a few thousand years if what we know of Gravity is true throughout the universe (there is no reason for it not to be true that man is aware of). Therefore; logically—the universe can only be a few thousand years old. Evolution's claims of many billions of years of age violates this Law. The best known Creator account agrees with the evidence in the universe claiming only thousand of years of age.

6. **Law of Biogenesis**: The most proved Law of all Laws of Nature: <u>Life can **ONLY** come from pre-existing life</u>. Louis Pasteur proved the evolutionary Law of Spontaneous Generation *incorrect* <u>more than 125 years ago</u>. Still: The claim is made that life 'arose' on the 'early Earth' billions of years ago when it rained on the rocks for millions of years and formed a 'soup' of lifeless chemicals that then somehow 'came alive'. The so-called 'Primordial Soup' experiments actually prove that even with carefully controlled conditions—life from a collection of lifeless chemicals is IMPOSSIBLE! Many analyses of the data show the amino acids formed were of the wrong 'handedness' to allow life. Life from non-life is another lie being promoted as truth in the 7th and 10th grades to unsuspecting children and too-busy-to-check-it-out parents.

7. **Law of Increasing Entropy**: Called the premiere Law of the Universe by Albert Einstein—it states: Disorder rises in all systems. <u>Only the presence of intelligent purpose can bring order out of chaos</u>. Creation proponents credit the Creator with bringing the incredible order we observe in the universe into being. Evolutionists demand we believe all this order came about by sheer chance—they ask us to believe something that is impossible *just because they say it is so*. <u>We will not</u>!!

8. **Law of Electromagnetism**: The Earth has a magnetic field. Where did it come from? Creation advocates credit the Creator with installing this essential feature for life in the only known planet designed for life. Evolutionists again try to make theoretical claims regarding the center of the Earth which they have never seen; neither have they demonstrated that their ideas would even result in a magnetic field—yet they demand we believe them without question or proof. Why should anyone simply give away their mind in this manner? Not us! We will be thinking and reasoning persons. We will believe common sense Creation explanations.

9. **Law of Layer Deposition**: This Law basically states that in a pile of dirt/rock that has laid around undisturbed—logically we should find the oldest objects (those first laid down) near the bottom. However; unless the deposition of the pile was observed historically by a credible witness—<u>NO length of time can be assigned to the object deposition</u>; only logic can be used to give an indication of the events that led to the objects being where they are. If human made objects (termed OOPARTS—Out Of Place ARTifactS) are found in layers supposedly hundreds of millions or billions of years old—logically: Evolution's time scale of billions of years IS disproven—or else dinosaurs and trilobites made and used tools!

10) This Law will yield many theses of the 95 total; as follows: A metal alloy hammer with wood handle was found in 1926 in the 'Cretaceous' (chalk) layer. This layer is where the vast majority of dinosaur fossils are found and is believed by evolutionists to be hundreds of millions of year old. Take your pick—either these layers were deposited rapidly by a vast flood of waters or dinosaurs made and used tools. Hmmm . . . I remember an account of a Flood from somewhere . . .

11) A gold chain was found in a lump of coal from a layer supposedly 450 million years old—a layer populated primarily by trilobites and such.

12) A brass bell also found in a lump of coal

13) A stone figure found in a deep core drilling

14) Dinosaur footprints found only 4 feet deep in Illinois in 2007

15) Footprint of dinosaur stepping on a human footprint in Texas near the Paluxy River

16) A fossilized human finger from layers where dinosaur fossils were also found

17. **Supposed Missing Mass**: As stated: Galaxies could not exist in their current shapes according to Evolution unless there is 90% more mass than known to exist. A true scientist would accept the most logical explanation that fits the evidence: A Creator. Evolutionists attempt to find the missing mass by impossible-to-prove entities such as Black Holes/Dark Energy/Dark Mass—concepts never observed and which are bandages to make the Evolution mantra believable for the uninformed. These scientists have no trouble believing in unseen entities unless such a belief means they are responsible and accountable for their life to the unseen Creator! It is their desire to not have to give account for their lives to the Creator that drives their insane promotion of the lie of Evolution.

More from the universe:

18. **Comet orbits**: Since much of the comet's mass burns away each orbit (forming the 'tail' we see)—it can logically only make so many trips around before it is completely burned up. These 'short term comets'—even those like the famous Halley's comet with an orbit taking it near our sun every 80+ years could only be a few thousand years old since it is still here. That there are still short-term comets tells us the

universe is only thousands of years old (agrees with Creation accounts) while Evolution has <u>no scientific mechanism</u> to explain these comets.

19. **Comet origins**: We know comets cannot last but a few thousand years: Evolution adherents must come up with a source (creation advocates claim the Creator is the source; very logical and plausible). As with Black Holes/Dark Energy—they make up provably incorrect mechanisms for short term comets such as being belched from volcanoes on nearby planets or the 'Oort Cloud' (a conveniently unobserved belt of comets just outside our solar system). Think about it: If the Oort Cloud existed—our telescopes would have to look THROUGH it to get the pictures of farther off galaxies—why would we not be able to get evidence it really exists? It is another unprovable claim— actually: A lie.

20. **Comet trajectories**: Even it the Oort Cloud did exist; there is no known mechanism for short-term comets to simply 'fall' into the stable orbits they are observed to have. Creation proponents have no such dilemma—the Creator placed these comets into their orbits at the Creation of the universe—as a sign to those who need a sign to recognize the work of a Creator.

21. **Comet and Star destruction**: Recently we observed a comet hit Jupiter—destroying the comet. We have observed star destruction—nova and supernova. We have never observed either star or comet birth. Creation claims the Creator made the stars and by extension everything in the universe. Evolution vainly purports unproved concepts for comets and equally unproved 'gas/dust-cloud' condensation stories for star births. A pattern of asking us to believe a lot of things without a shred of proof is evident on the evolutionist side of the fence—and yet they call creation believers 'religious' while claiming they are scientific!

22. **Our moon**: Rocks brought back from our moon show a different physical make-up than our planet. The main Evolution idea was that our Moon was belched out from our Earth—could not have happened! Evolutionists have no explanation for the origin of our moon. Creation adherents do have an explanation—the Creator made it and put it in orbit as a witness to the Creator.

23. **Our moon**: Slowly escaping from Earth's orbit—which means it used to be closer. If Evolution's timescale of hundreds of millions of years were true—the moon would have TOUCHED the earth just a few million years ago. Evolution is WRONG! Since the moon causes the tides on Earth; massive flooding twice a day would have occurred in the supposed millennia past.

24. **Our moon**: Craters have very sharp features. Gravity should have pulled these down quite a lot if it had been acting for Evolution's supposed billions of years. The same effect is seen on Earth in old building's glass—thicker at the bottom than at the top. Though the glass is 'solid'—it still flows.

25. **Our moon's orbit**: The shape of our moon's orbit defies explanation by evolutionists; but the Creator could do it just to give proof of Creation. The Creator desires for man to know the truth—and left evidence since the Creator is not visible to man's eyes. {See Lumpy Oatmeal with Raisins and Cinnamon for explanation of the unseen Reality of the Creator at PublishAmerica.com}

26. **Venus' largest Mountain**: The surface of Venus is hot enough to melt lead—yet this mountain was shown by our spacecraft to still have very defined and sharp features inconsistent with millions of years but perfectly consistent with Creation ideas of a YOUNG universe on the order of a few thousand years old.

27. **Meteor belt**—Evolution supposes our rocky Earth is made up of meteors that 'caught up with each other' somehow

and melted together over a billion years (of course no one saw this happen; we are simply to believe it without proof). If true; logically—there should be more planets forming in the meteor belt or be no meteor belt left if the same effects that formed our planet were in effect just a few million miles away. Creation adherents believe the Creator made the planets—and the comets—and the meteors: Perfectly logical without mental gymnastics.

28. **Galaxy rotation**: Many galaxies show rotation that has only been occurring for a few thousand years based on our measurements of their rate of rotation. Either these galaxies were recently created (Creation model) or Evolution must come up with a way to birth not only stars (which they have not) but entire groupings of billions of stars.

29. **Inconsistent moons of Jupiter**: Moons around the planets should logically have formed under the same conditions and should be very similar: Yet—Io is volcanic and its neighbor is an iceball. Io cannot have been sitting out in the absolute zero of space for even tens of millions of years and retain its heat without some kind of heat input. It is a fact of Physics! Evolutionists guess the source may be Jupiter's gravitational push/pull but then fail to apply it to ALL of Jupiter's moons equally. Creationists of course have no such problem—the Creator was leaving evidence of Creation for us to find!

30. **Depth of moon dust**: In 1969; our astronauts were worried they would sink into a projected very deep layer of moon dust—because they were told the moon had been up there billions of years and our other spacecraft had measured a very dusty solar system. They found only a few thousand years worth of dust when they actually got there. Creationists must have got there first to clean up the landing spot to deceive the evolutionists—yeah, right.

31. **Great distances in space**: The limits of our instruments and measuring methods is only about 600 light years. After this distance—**all distances are a guess**; but are purported

to be fact. All the talk about billions and billions of light years proving the great age of the universe is just that: Talk—no one knows; except the Creator. Again; we see the evolutionists withhold critical information about the universe to keep people believing in their impossible story.

32. **Our sun' burn rate**: Our sun burns an estimated 5 million tons of fuel a minute. That fuel has to take up space. If our sun had been burning for even millions of years—the planet Mercury would not exist, nor would Venus—and Earth would have been a baked rock for the supposed billions of years that life was 'evolving'. Evolution is a fairy tale for adults.

Enough with outer space—let us get down to Earth!

33. **Law-breaking sequences of events for Evolution**: First something came from nothing; then Law of Gravity defying planet formation occurred; then somehow rain came about and formed a soup; then somehow the soup came alive; then one celled critters grew legs and crawled up on land; then for some reason apes won the struggle for survival and decided to shave—and here we are! Author Frank Perretti quipped that this sounds like: From Goo to You by way of the Zoo!

34. **Violations of the Law of Entropy**: Every time life supposedly crawled up to the next step of the ladder— numerous biological changes would have been required. This means new, never before existing information for DNA codes had to come about by sheer chance—in complete and utter violation of the Law of Entropy. We have discovered that DNA and cells are many, many times more complex than our most modern (intelligently designed and manufactured) computers!

35. **Mathematics of impossibility**: The accepted odds that make an event impossible are one in ten to the 150th power. The calculated odds of the 100 protein chains that make up the most 'simple' bacteria coming about by sheer evolutionary chance is more than 1 in ten to the $3,000,000,000^{th}$ power.

By evolutionists own projections—chance formation of this 'simple' bacteria is absolutely IMPOSSIBLE. *Molecules-to-man Evolution simply did not happen*. It is a politically inspired lie of Marxists and the power behind Marxism—designed to attempt to dethrone the Creator (which will not work—long term).

36. **Mathematics of possibility**: When discussing opposite concepts such as Evolution and Creation—evidence against one is also evidence for the other. The reciprocal of the odds of impossibility are the odds the opposite is true. In other words—the odds of Creation being true are over ten to the 3,000,000,000th power to one. Again: Evidence against Evolution is also evidence for the opposite view of Creation. I really like those odds!!

37. **Atomic structure**: As one very familiar with Nuclear Theory formally approved by the U.S. Nuclear Regulatory Commission: Protons are positively charged and in the nucleus. The electrostatic repulsion between these protons is more than ten to the 40th power as great as the gravitational attraction due to the mass of the protons. The atom as we know it should not exist. When asked what holds atoms together; Enrico Fermi (the 'Father of Nuclear Power) is purported to have said, "As far as I can tell—spirit!" A man who was responsible for the most incredible technology could not explain how it works without appealing to a Creator!

38. **Nuclear force**: The theoretical force (not-able-to-be-proved-but-must-exist) that holds the nucleus of an atom together is the only field force that does not act exponentially (gets rapidly less with distance). It operates full force to a short distance then drops to nearly zero. Electrostatic repulsion decays exponentially. If the graphs of the two forces are superimposed on each other—it can be shown that the only way for atoms to exist as we understand them to exist is for the protons to be purposefully pushed together to a point where the nuclear force will hold them together. <u>This</u>

means EVERY atom above hydrogen in the universe had to be ASSEMBLED. Talk about an ALMIGHTY Creator!!

39. **Earth's elements no-where else**: Of all the elements known to man—only on Earth are nearly all known to be present! How strange if the universe came about by random processes that any place in the universe would have all and no other place would have all of them. A Creator with a purpose for the Earth would solve this mystery—wouldn't it?

40. **Polonium radio-halos**: The work of Dr. Gentry has shown that the Earth's foundational granites had to have been formed essentially instantaneously and not by cooling from magma over millions or even a single year. The radioactive decay of Polonium left circular patters that could not have existed in this shape if the decay occurred while the rock were liquid and able to move. The very short decay time of Polonium and the circular shape prove the rock was formed very quickly. The evolutionists have no explanation for this and so do not talk about it—and have expelled Dr. Gentry from their circles. How very tolerant of them.

41. **Heavy elements**: There is no known natural mechanism to get to the higher elements except alpha decay. There is a block to this mechanism at the element Technetium which has not been found to exist naturally on Earth. The mechanism of beta minus decay (a neutron turns into a proton by giving up an electron) to make a higher element (greater proton count) is blocked by the missing Technetium. How then did we get Uranium, Plutonium, etc? A Creator in the picture solves this problem—Evolutionists appeal to unknown, non-scientific supposed effects of the Big Bang—but they aren't religious in appealing to unobserved forces are they? Ha!

42. **Too little Helium**: The heavy elements spontaneously break down by a process called 'alpha' decay. An alpha particle is a Helium atom stripped of its electrons. There are only a few thousand year's worth of Helium in the Earth's

atmosphere. A person may believe a worm can become a man in millions of years—but if you say it happened in just thousands of years they laugh. Yet the Earth is scientifically provable to be only thousands of years old.

43. **Niagra Falls**: The rate of erosion of the falls has been about 5 feet a year. At this rate—if the Falls were even 11,000 years old; it would have eroded back to the Great Lake preceding it! Obviously—the Falls are only a couple thousand years old. I have pictures of the Falls from the late 1800s—the famous 'U' shape observed today because of this erosion is just beginning.

44. **Coral reefs too small**: The largest coral reef in the world is the Great Barrier Reef off Australia. A portion of it was destroyed and a group studied its recovery. Based on this evidence; this group (not known for being Creation friendly by the way) calculated the age of the reef to be only about 4000 years old.

45. **Oldest living organism**: The oldest known living thing is a tree on California's coast. It is estimated to be about 4000 years old. Why are there no older living things if the Earth is supposedly billions of years old? The Earth is NOT billions of years old! It was created by a Creator that had a purpose in mind for it.

46. **Sahara Desert too small**: Deserts grow as the prevailing winds blow across them. A group determined the world's largest desert is only about 4000 years old. Why does everything appear to point to some significant event about 4000 years ago? What was that event? It is hard to have a desert under a Flood. There is an account of a worldwide Flood about 4000 years ago. Must be just co-incidence.

47. **Wooly Mammoths**: Incorrectly and deceivingly named— the 'wooly mammoth' had hair consistent with WARM climates. Yet there are tusks from such critters all over the Arctic Circle—indicating a population of some 5 million.

How could such a desolately cold climate (today) have supported such a population?

48. **Saguaro Cactus**: Apparently native ONLY to the desert southwestern United States—the desert where they are found was apparently a lush grassland just a few thousand years ago—and mammoth remains are found there. How could something so odd as the Saguaro 'evolve' in such a short period of time. The National Park guide told us it evolved from a leafy shrub—but she could not tell me exactly how; just that it did. Why should I believe this?

49. **Erosion rates of mountains**: Based on the current erosion rate of Earth's mountains—they will all erode flat in just 11 million years. How then can they still be here—and well defined—if the Earth is billions of years old? The Earth is only thousands of years old. Oh, yeah—fossils that are supposedly hundreds of millions of years old are found on those mountains. How is that possible if the mountains could not have existed for even 20 million years? The earth is YOUNG! Evolutionists keep making up more time to calm the fears of those they have deceived—in the 1920s the earth was said to be only ten million years old, in the 1800s it was only 2-3 million years old. How often do they get to be wrong before we get to stop believing them?

50. **Clams on Mt. Everest!**: As the comic strip B.C. quipped, 'Clams have feet!'—they must have them to get to the top of Everest (and every other mountain range for that matter) before men did. Fossilized marine life forms are found at the tops of all Earth's mountain ranges. The other possibility it that the Earth really was covered with water at one time (a world-wide Flood).

51. **Salinity of oceans**: Currently only about 18,000 parts per million salt. If the oceans were once pure water and using today's very slow rate of salt build-up; the current 18,000 ppm could be reached in just about 1 million years using standard concentration and dilution chemical equations.

This means the oceans—where life supposedly evolved some 500 million years ago—are not nearly old enough for Evolution to be true. Evolution is scientifically and logically disproved. If the oceans did not start out pure water and one takes into accounts a worldwide Flood that erupted from subterranean chambers and some passed through salt layers: Today's level of salt can be reached in just thousands of years.

52. **Mineral and Delta build-up**: Salt is not the only thing that washes into the oceans and stays there. Many different minerals and simple mud does as well. In each case; there are not nearly enough minerals in the oceans or large enough deltas at the point of major rivers entering the ocean to believe that the oceans are but a few thousand years old. Amoebae to man in a few thousand years?—no.

53. **Salt unravels DNA**: Tomato DNA can be stripped out and 'unwound' by adding a little salt to the water containing blended tomato. The salt neutralizes the electric charge that binds the DNA molecule tightly together. This is a common science experiment—but also proves a cell's tightly bound DNA strand could never have formed in a 'warm salty ocean' of long ago. The only way for the DNA packed into a cell to have occurred is for a Creator to have packed it.

54. **Missing Chain not Missing Link**: A close study of the imagined 'Linage of Mankind' shows each and every one to be either an outright fraud or a very biased interpretation. Evolutionists are not looking for a Missing Link to finally form the line—they have neither a starting point nor an end point—and they know it! There is, however, big grant money and academic praise for those who keep the faith and offer ever wilder tales of how it all might have come about. This is why they stick together and ridicule creationists—in the Mafia it is called 'Omerta'—the Dons of Evolution academically execute any brave enough to rat on them.

55. **Lucy**—Dr. Johanson found the remains in two discoveries: Half of it was hundreds of feet below the other half and more than a mile away from each other. He then combined the remains and called the critters one critter—made up a good story and is now making hundreds of thousands of dollars a year regaling his stories to mush-brained kids in a university sent there by unsuspecting parents. No sane person would conclude these two finds were the same critter.

56. **Nebraska man**—This one was based on a single tooth; which was later discovered to be a pig when excavated further. When the error was revealed—did the evolutionists correct the record publicly? No—it was left to the creationists to try to inform the public at large of the error and follow-on deception.

57. **Java man**—The remains of a large gibbon apparently. The discoverer was a rabid Evolutionist looking for evidence. We will never know for sure: The fossils have been conveniently lost.

58. **Piltdown man**—An outright fraud. Again; the evolutionists did not correct the record; but to the contrary have done everything they can to perpetuate the lie.

59. **Neanderthal man**—Named for the Neander valley in Germany where it was found—this was simply a man suffering from severe arthritis and rickets.

60. **Cro-magnon man**—Admitted by Evolutionists: If you dressed him up today—no one would know the difference—so any difference is only in the minds of evolutionists.

61. **Fluffy the Cat**: Fluffy was one of those neighborhood strays. It got killed by a car; rotted on the roadside until dry and crispy. I interred Fluffy's remains so I could ask folks about Fluffy. After a few questions, it became obvious that those who did not know of Fluffy's life by direct observation could only guess about her life. What did she eat? Did she

have kids? Were the kids mutated in some way? Could there ever be a mutation that would instinctively tell stray cats not to run out in front of cars? The same is true of the fragmented pieces of bones found in the desert. All the evolutionists can do is make claims about these creatures that they NEVER observed in life—they CANNOT know anything for sure about them. Why am I not allowed to believe what I want about them? A wonderful book called Behold Now Behemoth!—Dinosaurs All Over the Bible is available on Amazon.com. It appears man and dinosaur have always lived together!

62. **Fossils show NO evolution**: Many creatures supposed to be tens or hundreds of millions of years old—and extinct—have been found alive! A so-called fossil tree is being cultivated in southeast Asia. The Coelacanth (living fossil fish) was thought extinct for 70 million years—then found alive and unevolved off the coasts of India. Yet during those imagined 70 million years—man is claimed to have gone from a lemur to what we are today. Someone is WRONG—it is the evolutionists! I have a scorpion encased in fossilized amber supposedly fifty million years old. I have another scorpion I killed in my living room in October 2008—the two are exactly alike! No evolution for them while man changes so much? How can that be? Easy—it isn't true!!

63. **Fossils show sudden appearance**: By evolutionists own admission—the fossil record shows SUDDEN appearance of ALL vertebrates with NO valid transitional fossils ever discovered. All such claims of transitional forms have been debunked when allowed to be analyzed. Evolutionists have a lot of explaining to do—but they simply insult and call creationists 'fanatics'—are not the true fanatics those who believe their story IN SPITE of the factual evidence?

64. **Radiometric dating methods**: Shown to be unreliable for several reasons. First; the person doing the dating has to make assumptions. Those assumptions are based on the person's belief system. If the results do not match the pre-

existing belief system—the results are discarded! What sense does that make? The next several points will be examples of debunked radiometric dating—remember that I work in the nuclear industry and so I do know this material very well. Even with laboratory controls the results often have to be repeated to be verified.

65. **Radioactive element leaching**: The isotopes used in dating rocks can leach out of the sample. Since the sample was not controlled in a laboratory for its entire existence—there is no way the researcher can know that some of the measured substance did not leach out. If some did; the sample would APPEAR older—perhaps much older—than it really is.

66. **Lava from Hawaii**: Known to be only 200 years old was incorrectly dated to be over 100 million years old by a laboratory famous for its previous work in this field. Most laboratories will no longer date samples submitted by creationist groups—fearing that they will be similarly shown to be WRONG and lose their credibility. Sorry to 'out' you guys—but the Truth must be known!

67. **Living clams**: Carbon dated to be 2200 years old.

68. **Woolly mammoth skin**: Dated to be a few thousand years old and the wood upon which it rested when found dated to be tens of thousands of years old.

69. **Chemistry**: Defies evolutionary accounts of Earth's formation. There are no know explanations for the thick layers of salt found all around the Earth from an evolutionary perspective. The two base elements of common salt are sodium and chlorine; both in their pure form are lethal to human life—yet when put into a solution of water; they separate and yet neither is lethal! Indeed, the Creator knew we would need salt to live—and gave it to us in a form that would not hurt us. There are many, many chemical conundrums that evolutionists can't explain.

70. **Chemistry**: Automatically behaves in a very predictable, stable and orderly pattern in tens of millions of ways—all of which speaks of *an amazingly intelligent Chemist*; not of random evolutionary chance reactions.

71. **Biology**: The extraordinary complexity found in ALL living things speaks of *a supremely intelligent Biologist*; not some undirected process that has no purpose. Evolutionists can only lamely say the complexity we see is the 'appearance of' complexity—utter foolishness! I don't have to see the watch designer to know that there had to be a designer. Humans are much more complex than watches—and are ALIVE!

72. **Chicken-or-the-Egg-First scenarios**: Many situations exist where there is no logical choice but to conclude that the only solution to the problem is to admit a Creator was involved. Birds—Literally the supreme example of Chicken-or-the-Egg-First. If you say a Creator is responsible—you conclude the Chicken was created first having the ability pre-programmed into it to produce eggs—perfectly sound reasoning; mystery solved. The evolutionist cannot explain either without simply asking you to take his word for it because he is a self-proclaimed 'expert'.

73. **Extinction**: We are able to document the extinction of organisms but we never observe the establishment of new organisms. By 'new organisms' I mean totally new creatures; not the small changes between existing organisms that we do periodically see. The small horizontal changes are a fact; but ARE NOT the Evolution that supposedly causes molecules-to-man to be possible—that is called vertical evolution. The two are worlds apart and that one happens DOES NOT imply the other must have happened.

74. **Established barriers to interbreeding**: A cat cannot breed with a dog to create a 'Cag' or a 'Dat', etc. A bird cannot breed with a fish to create a 'firsh' or a 'birsh'. This happens all the time in science FICTION movies and is claimed to happen in so-called science books for public

schools. If man evolved from apes—why then do we still have apes? I thought 'Survival of the Fittest' meant lesser fit creatures died out? Remember: 'Survival of the Fittest' DOES NOT explain 'Arrival of the Fittest'.

75. **Non-beneficial, lethal mutations**: Vastly outnumber those so-called beneficial mutations which really are not; but just more examples of horizontal evolution (adaptation in many cases where it happens to succeed and not kill the offspring). Mutated animals are most often sterile. Bacteria that survive a new anti-biotic ALREADY had the information in their DNA—thus if they then multiply; no new information was generated via mutation; only the preservation of information that allowed that bacteria to live. Such survival can just as easily be explained in terms of a Creator wanting to ensure the survival of a basic kind of bacteria.

76. **Exclusive foods needed**: Some critters such as the Koala Bear must have a certain food or they perish. This means the if Evolution were true—we would have to believe that blind chance brought into existence—at the same time—in the same place—for no purpose whatsoever—two distinct living organisms. This is absurd on its face!

77. **Symbiotic relationships**: Similar to the argument above—many of these relationships exist and if they did not; the one or both organisms die. Both 76 & 77 were done by the Creator to give testimony to the Creator's existence—but Evolutionists cannot see the forest for the trees.

78. **Transfer of information**: The monarch butterfly is born in Canada, flies to and dies in Mexico. Their offspring having never made the flight back to Canada but somehow know the way! How did they know the way when they were never shown?

79. **Another transfer of information**: Salmon born to one generation know to migrate to the sea and back again where ALL the adults die. The next generation somehow knows

to do the same thing. Where did the pre-programmed information for 78 & 79 come from? If any point of information transfer along the way were messed up; the critter would die and the species would disappear. The information had to have been PRE-PROGRAMMED!

80. **DNA & RNA**: Probably the most complex chicken-or-egg mystery to evolutionists. DNA cannot be made without RNA and RNA cannot exist without an organism's DNA to make it. DNA could not have arisen in some warm pond as demonstrated earlier; nor could it make itself. Evolutionists tread water on this one saying, "It may take another 100 years to figure out how mindless, purposeless Evolution did this."—and expect us to be satisfied with this little 'pat-on-the-head-go-away-you-creationist-pest' stall. Sorry, we are NOT going away! You demand answers of us—we give them. Turn about is fair play! How did blind chance make organism's DNA vastly superior to our super computers?

81. **Care for weaker organisms**: Humans—the supposed pinnacle of evolution—routinely care for those who offer little or no survival value to their and other species. I gave my kidney to my wife who could no longer bear children. Why do such a thing that offers me no chance to 'pass on my genes' to more children—the supposed driver of all actions. Indeed; if my wife died—there would be the chance to remarry and father more children. This trait of humans and some animals is another mystery to evolutionists—it throws a wrench into their 'Survival of the Fittest by Tooth and Claw' mantra.

82. **Bird fossils**: Bird fossils have been found at the same level and layer as the dinosaurs they supposedly evolved from. Obviously the claim is false: Birds suddenly appear in the fossil record just as dinosaurs do. Birds have always been birds and dinosaurs have always been dinosaurs. Creation is the only explanation. Many 'feathered dinosaur' fossils have been exposed a frauds—but again; it is left to the Creationists to broadcast the error.

83. **Horse sequence**: The supposed 'horse sequence' of evolution is a complete lie. It has been exposed that the sequence is misrepresented according to which came first or existed at the same time as another supposed predecessor. The lies of evolution are completely out of control.

84. **Pepper moth 'beneficial' mutation**: The 'experiment' has now been admitted as faked. Even if it had been actually observed—all that was demonstrated as the black phase of the same moth became dominate in the areas around the factories that stained the trees dark with soot was: Horizontal adaptation of the same moth! No new information was present—only selection of information in the DNA of the moths already present. Creation agrees with this so-called 'horizontal evolution' which is really better called adaptation—the concept of 'Survival of the Fittest' was first proposed by a Creation believing man— then it was perverted by Evolutionists. This event cannot be extrapolated as scientific evidence for vertical, molecules-to-man Evolution.

85. **Fossil detail**: Very many fossils are found that depict the organism in extremely fine detail—does it really make any sense that such fossilization took place over millions of years? The soft structures would decay within hours or days and never be fossilized. At best we would have only bones, teeth or shells and possibly tree trunks. Fossilization had to be very rapid to cut off the oxygen and protect the corpse from scavengers and bacteria. I found a fossil dinosaur footprint that shows the toenails of the creature in exacting detail—how could that have survived for many millions of years. I am lucky it survived the few thousands of years that it did.

86. **Fossil leaves**: Even the veins of the leaves are shown in detail. These fossils are extremely rare in natural rock; but I did find one in my backyard. A glob of cement used on my pool fell on a leaf and imprinted it—then the leaf decayed away. That imprint fossil was obviously accomplished in a

few hours. Hear this: Fossils then **ARE NOT** an indicator of long ages of time—but of SPECIAL CONDITIONS such as wet cement or in nature; mud.

87. **Geology**: Many examples from geology contradict evolution's claims and at the same time support the Creation position. The Grand Canyon is one—how do you get water to flow uphill?—unless there is great pressure behind it. Topographical mappings from space clearly show that the now drained Grand Lake once covered nearly 3 western States. At the opening of Grand Canyon there is a narrow funnel-like gorge about 800 feet deep—I have stood right at the edge of it. The water from Grand Lake had been stopped by this natural dam but apparently broke through and thundered along cutting Grand Canyon in a matter of days and carrying the sandy sediments across modern day Arizona wiping out the grasslands, burying mammoths and creating a desert where the Saguaro cactus apparently survived. Everything works with Creation explanations!

88. **Grand Canyon's layers**: Are missing something if they formed over millions of years: Meteorites! A certain percentage of meteors survive to crash into Earth—and it logically follows that some of them would be found in the layers of Grand Canyon at a predictable rate if those famous layers were laid down slowly. None have been found—this is anecdotal indication the layers were laid down rapidly.

89. **Mars Flood**: In exploring Mars—large geologic formations very similar to Earth have been found. The scientist's explanation?—a planetary sized flood! Why could it happen on Mars but be so impossible on Earth. The average height of land above sea level is only about 2000 feet. The average depth of the oceans is more than 5000 feet. If the Earth were perfectly smooth—it would right now be covered with over a half mile of water!

90. **Water source for a world-wide flood**: At the bottom of every ocean are UPWARD fissures that show up on

maps of the ocean floor like seams on a baseball. The evolution ruling junta has no explanation for them—but the Creationists do: There is a famous account of the 'fountains of the great deep being broken up' which resulted in the inundation of the Earth. Just because some do not like this historical account of the power of the Creator does not mean it is not true. Men then were accountable to the Creator, this has not changed.

91. **Mount St. Helens**: Proves massive geological gorges and valley can be cut in a very short time. After the eruption; Spirit Lake was dammed up by the debris until it broke through and cut a canyon 1/40th the size of Grand Canyon in just 3 days. The layering was identical to Grand Canyon and the small creek left at the end of the cutting is just what is seen on a larger scale at Grand Canyon.

92. **Mount St. Helens also**: Showed the snapping off of trees which ended up in Spirit Lake. The floating logs debarked each other as they were blown about by the wind. The bark has formed a layer on the lake bottom and appears to be turning into coal! We have a good indication of how the massive coal deposits were formed by a world-wide Flood on Earth. As logs became water-logged; they tipped upright and sank into the silt and mud bottom. This process demonstrated perfectly how the numerous polystrate fossil trees (fossil trees extending through numerous layers) were formed rapidly and NOT over millions of years.

93. **Mount Vesuvius**: Buried the town of Pompeii in ash and lava. Many residents were killed and fossilized in a few minutes. If we had not known of this eruption from historical records—evolutionists wedded to the idea of millions of years would have told us this happened over millions of years. Rediculous!

94. **Evolution's Monkeys and Typewriters analogy**: A supreme masquerade in the long and dubious search for anything at all that might appear to be serious reasoning in

support of Evolution's claim of the power of chance. It is said a million monkeys hammering away on typewriters for a million years would by chance type every great literary work. Excuse me—but the chimps would have to be fed, supplied with paper and ink, kept at their job by someone and most of all: The typewriters are created objects as is the language the chimps are ignorant of. If this is scientific reasoning—we are in serious trouble! The Creator made everything and gave us the intelligence to make things ourselves.

95. **Finally**: Even the Evolution community DOES NOT really believe in Evolution when you get them talking among themselves: They do HOPE it is true; but they do not really believe it is. One of their prime defenders characterized the odds of Evolution being true as LESS LIKELY than the chance of a 747 jetliner being assembled by a tornado rampaging through a junkyard. Who is believing against the odds in a religious way here? Creationists are supremely confident in their concepts because as has been shown here—the FACTS and LOGIC are on our side.

Though there are many, many more examples of the utter failure of Evolution to explain the actual data—these 95 theses will suffice to wake up the open-minded reader who actually wants the Truth to shake off the mind-chains of Evolution and be freed to the truth of Creation. Darwinism is the foundation of Atheism and Atheism is the foundation of Marxism. Now a few words directed to Darwinists and Atheists.

EVERY disastrous idea that has plagued mankind can be traced back to a rejection of the Creator. Communism, Socialism, Racism and Slavery, Sexism, Abortion are just a few of the horrors Evolutionists are responsible for. Hitler, Stalin, Pol Pot and Mao were Evolutionists that unfortunately had the power of the State on their side. More than 100,000,000 human murders are on their records. Another 50,000,000 abortions worldwide will be held to account one day. Tens of millions of enslaved souls have cried out for their Creator granted freedom across the centuries but you kept them in chains. Women have been denied equality by you because your hero Charles Darwin claimed them to be inferior to you. Know this: The Truth will always prevail—and you are purveyors of a lie!

There is a Creator that can forgive even all of this wickedness. You know which one I am talking about. It is strongly recommended you avail yourself of this option BEFORE you face the One Who made you. You only have as long as you draw breath—the very breath the Creator put into you—to admit what you have been doing and turn from it. Like it or not: Your belief system has been NUKED and you know it. Replace it with the TRUTH before it is too late.

The portion of this book called The 95 Theses may be freely copied, printed, transmitted and translated. All of the rest of the book Behold Now Behemoth: Dinosaurs All Over the Bible! is covered by its copyright statement with all rights reserved. Please send the 95 Theses everywhere you can by any and all means possible. Publicity is the surest way to break the power of deceit which has reigned in mankind's minds for far too long.

A poem honoring the countless Christian martyrs through the ages.

One slave girl named Blandia is called out in these verses; representing all that have stood bravely for Christ against despots and tyrants through the ages.

This poem was released by the author of Behold Now Behemoth: Dinosaurs All Over the Bible!—to the Internet's Public Domain prior to publication of this book. As such, this poem may be freely copied, used and transmitted. The rest of the book is covered by the Copyright statement with all rights reserved.

Confessor Today?
by Glenn L. Wilson

As I stir my designer coffee,
settling into my reclining chair,
Turning on a lamp, so I can better see,
remotely adjusting conditioning of the air,
I open the ancient martyr book,
purchased from an on-line store,
In an instant am transported back to look,
at the time of the true Christian confessor,

Blandia!—a slave: For what did she suffer so?;
"The Name of Christ!", I read,
For in Rome two thousand years ago,
a capital crime was it merely to believe . . . .
The capricious 'gods' of Empire Rome,
could bear to have no rival,
One Who made master and slave,
men and women—all before Christ: Equal!

"They must be killed!—and horribly so!
An example to one and all!
"Swear 'Caesar is God!'—or off you go,
to the arena where you will fall!"
With dozens more, Blandia heard her fate,
"Fed alive to beasts or burned!"
Dragged through that gate,
"Deny Christ and live!"—an option, she did learn . . .

Those watching her torture greatly marveled,
as her torment went on three days,
'til short Roman sword their blood-lust filled,
still!—no denial did Blandia raise.
It is said of even that hardened crowd,
"No woman ever suffered so!"
Then breaking trance, I reached out,
to find my latte had grown stone cold.

The stories of thousands more rolled on,
for centuries right up 'til today,
Tyrants freely shedding righteous seed-corn
blood—for God alone they would obey,
"Lord Jesus! Please forgive my sin!
When Your witness I am shy to be,
"Tomorrow before my skeptic 'friends',
 put Blandia's boldness deep in me!"

Other works by Glenn L. Wilson

The Write In—by Erik Alden (pen name):

A religious / political fictional story of a Christian man that gets elected to the Presidency of the United States by Write In vote—and turns Washington upside down!

Available at PublishAmerica.com and other distributors

Lumpy Oatmeal with Raisins . . . *and Cinnamon!*— *Reintroducing the Christian Church to Her Supernatural God*:

A Christian apologetics book that 'gives permission' to people to believe again in the God clearly described in the Bible. In our so-called, 'Age of Science!'—many folks do not understand that it is actually the Bible that agrees with true science and the evolutionists that are completely wrong about how to interpret the evidence.

Contains a special section in the back: The original 95 Theses Proving Evolution is a Lie!—powerful ammunition for those seeking to defend God's Word cover to cover.

Available at PublishAmerica.com and other distributors

The King James II Bible: Only the Words of God!

A special rendering of the King James Bible. Many special features not found in ANY English translation; such as:

No verse breaks—read the Bible as it was written, an unbroken sequence of thoughts. Verse breaks were added in the 1600s.

De-emphasized chapter breaks—again, added in the 1200s; but interrupts thoughts in progress.

All of God's Words in Red—in the Old Testament, God speaks a lot! The Holy Spirit has something to say as well. Now you can see Who says what and when.

Conversational paragraphing and punctuation with all italicized (added) words removed—leaving ONLY the Words of God. The first time EVER in the English language.

Currently available ONLY by e-mail: <u>kingjames2bible@gmail.com</u>—you will be given instructions for obtaining a copy at a cost of $20 to cover ($5 covers production and mailing; $15 will support missionaries across the globe).

For Bible researchers ONLY—provide to me your credentials and the reason you would like a copy of my King James II Bible with notations and an address. After checking you out via internet some—I will mail you a copy at my own expense to help you save time in figuring out some of the questions I have not been able to fathom. Whatever you discover; please be so kind as to let me know. Thank you in advance.

Glenn's Short List of Recommended Books and Organizations

Books:

1) <u>The Lie</u> by Ken Ham

2) <u>Tornado in a Junkyard</u> by James Perloff

3) <u>Buried Alive</u> by Jack Cuozzo

4) <u>How Could a Loving God . . . ?</u> by Ken Ham

5) <u>Under God</u> by Toby Mac and Michael Tait

6) <u>The Present Reign of Jesus Christ</u> by Robert Caringola

7) <u>Secrets of the Ica Stones</u> by Dennis Swift

8) <u>In The Beginning . . . .</u> by Dr. Walt Brown

9) <u>The Funky Tales of Ookachewbie</u> by Halita & Megan Wilson (hey, they are my daughters and this is their first book in the series—great for when you just need to laugh)

Organizations:

1) <u>Creation Science Evangelism</u>—Dr. Kent Hovind drdino.com

2) <u>Answers In Genesis</u>—Ken Ham answersingenesis.org

3) <u>Institute for Creation Research</u>—Dr. Morris

4) <u>Creation Evidence Museum</u>—Dr. Carl Baugh

5) <u>Center for Scientific Creation</u>—Dr. Walt Brown

The Biblical Basis for the Equality of Born-again People—specifically: Male / Female and so-called 'Races'

I was not going to include this chapter—being eager to just get this long-labored-over book to the publisher; but God laid it on my heart to at least briefly cover this topic. God wants to bring peace to all of humankind—and He is the only One that can do it; as the human race has proven to itself over and over again.

The only way for there to ever be true peace is for all people to embrace Real Truth—i.e. the Word of God. In the Bible are found the only Words of true Life and Peace and Healing—I capitalize these words because they must be 'not of human' origin to accomplish so lofty a feat. Peter recognized this fact when he said, 'Lord!—to Whom shall we go? You have the Words of Eternal Life!' For all the times Peter gets it wrong, this is one time he got it RIGHT!

Two of the most horribly twisted issues in this world today are the issues of male / female equality and racism. In most countries around this globe, women are treated as property or at best 'second class citizens'. Charles Darwin's extant writings indicate he believed women to be 'less evolved' than men. Also because of the lie of evolution, people have been led to believe there are more than one 'race' of humans—allowing for one to be superior to another—the very source of racism.

First, what does the Bible have to say about male / female equality? In the beginning, it is clearly recorded that Adam was made first, then the woman was carefully crafted. Did you catch that?—when Adam was 'made' (Strong's 6213-asah)—he was simply 'made' like the rest of the creation. When the woman was 'made'—we see that a different word is used (Strong's 1129-banah-to build, obtain children, repair).

God made the male man with a deficiency—and so in the second chapter of Genesis, He showed Adam all the mates for the animals—so that Adam would see that he had no similar mate created specially for him. God then creates a wombed man—a woman—to 'repair' Adam's deficiency—and give the ability to pro-create more humans.

Notice that 'man' in this sense is referred to in the global mankind meaning. God made male and female man—man as a 'kind'—mankind. The dominion mandate giving authority over the creation of God is given to both king Adam and queen Woman. There is not the slightest hint that this wombed man is to be considered anything less than fully equal in the sight of God, being a specially created 'help, meet for (Adam)'.

Adam was created first and Scripture records that he was told and shown things—specifically the creation of what is assumed to be the female animals out of the ground in Genesis chapter two. Adam also was the only one Scripture records as hearing the command of God not to eat of the tree of the knowledge of good and evil. For reasons known only to God, the woman was not shown the other animals as they were created. Adam therefore has more direct knowledge than the woman. More knowledge generally equates with greater responsibility.

We can assume Adam told her the story of the creation of the other animals and the command of God—and it even appears that Adam added to the command of God—because the woman misquotes what Adam must have told her that God had said. She apparently adds the part about 'neither shall ye touch it'. God did not say that to Adam—so one must draw a conclusion about why she said it; either she made it up on her own—or Adam added to the Command God had given him. In the New Testament, it is said that Eve was deceived, but Adam sinned with full knowledge. Adam is right there beside her when the serpent speaks to her—for right after taking the fateful bite, she turns to him and offers him the fruit.

This is why conscious sin is equated with Adam; while ignorant sin is attributed to the woman in the encounter with Nachash—the devil-inhabited serpent. Because Adam was created first and was given more knowledge—he occupies a unique place as the most responsible being in guarding the Truth and obeying God in leading his new family.

The importance of not adding to the Words of God is also painfully demonstrated—for the serpent seized upon the error—and Adam did not correct the record on the spot, but went along—knowing full well he was sinning.

As the Old Testament is the foundation and at the same time a shadow for the New Testament—we see that Jesus humbles Himself before God the Father—though They are equal to Each-Other! This 'equal partner submission' is identified by the word 'hupotasso (5293)' in Greek. It means to 'line up behind / under in support of' and presupposes that the one lining up behind / under is worthy of being followed! The woman lines up behind and in support of Adam; though they are equal with regard to personhood before God. She does this because—at that time—Adam was still lined up under / in support of God—and she is specially created to be his 'help, meet for him'.

Hupotasso is also the word used in the famously mistreated verse, 'Wives, submit to your husbands.' The word rendered 'submit' here in English is hupotasso (5293)—not (5298) hupochoreo;which means essentially to back down in silence or in recognition of authority. Married women are to line up in support of their godly husbands; just as the men are to line up in support of Jesus—the symbolic 'husband' of the Church. This is how families will best work and societies made up of godly families would prosper. The context where this passage is found DOES NOT address or limit a saved woman's activity in the community. Paul's letters and the Book of Acts contain many references to 'leading women' of Greek communities. Lydia was a business woman that befriended Paul.

If Paul was so down on women—why did he resort to the places where women were found in abundance—by the rivers where clothes were washed; water drawn and prayers offered? There are at least two reasons—probably first: There was no telephone or telegraph—so Paul chose the best way to get the word out in those days—the woman-to-woman network. Second—women have always been more spiritually sensitive than hard-headed men—and men generally do what their wives ask them to do—eventually. Paul had no doubt heard of Jesus speaking to the woman at the well in Samaria—who then brought the entire city of men to hear Him.

Most have probably noticed that I call Adam's 'help, meet for him' by the title 'Woman' thus far and not 'Eve'. That is because the Bible does the same thing up to Chapter 3. It is only after Adam is given dominion over the animals that he names some of them. In the Hebrew culture, naming something (or renaming it)shows one has been dominion over that thing. Eve got her name not from God—but from Adam immediately after God pronounces sentence on each of the three involved in the incident. Adam names her to demonstrate that part of the curse God places on her: The removal of her status as co-regent queen. God places her under the guidance of Adam instead of by his side as before—and Adam immediately names her.

Equality has been longed for—and fought for—ever since by women. Equality is offered twice to women in Scripture; once in the Old Testament to Hadassah (renamed Esther by the Babylonians that now had dominion over her) and once in the New Testament to the daughter of Herodias; illegal wife of Herod. In both settings, a king offers up to half his kingdom to the woman. Why half? Ten percent would have made them richer than their wildest dreams! Half was offered because it can reasonably be assumed that the offer was equality, not riches. The king was offering something not his to grant—for only the God-man Jesus, being equal with God Who put the curse in place, could remove it.

It would logically then follow that should the curse ever be removed by Someone equal with God—the daughters of Eve that inherited the curse (just as the sons of Adam inherited the curse of death that was similarly removed) could be restored to full co-regency! The only One that could do such a thing has already done it! Jesus dying on the Cross achieves more than just Salvation from death—as the verse stating that as He rose, He gave gifts to people. He is the 'second Adam'! He longs for His wife to be fully restored to queenship. His death reverses the entire curse put on mankind in the Garden!

A rough analogy is the recent wedding of Prince William to Kate Middleton. She was a 'commoner'!—and he will one day be the King of England. His status elevates her upon marriage to a position she could never have had on her own: Queen of England. All she could ever have hoped for had he not married her was to bow in his presence.

Now she is one with him and may produce princes and princesses that carry the 'royal blood'. Jesus has done the same thing for us! The one-day King of the Universe has deigned to take we sinners as His Bride—cleansing and elevating us to a position we could never have attained on our own.

Is this claim supported by Scripture? Yes! The word woman is used very many times in the Old Testament. It is word 802—'ishshah and simply means, 'a woman'. When this happens in word use—the only way to get an idea of what the word truly means is by looking at some important contexts. In every use AFTER the Garden of Eden incident; the context speaks of a being that is subjugated to the male of the human species. She is relegated to non-leadership roles UNLESS the men are unworthy of leading (Deborah in the Book of Judges) or she usurps the role (Athaliah, the only 'queen' of Judah). Even Sarah, Abraham's wife, is spoken of as calling Abraham 'lord'. The curse is firmly in place with women being treated about the same as cattle or other property—if not worse.

Some will say, 'But Paul in the New Testament won't let women even speak in church!'—again, we must look at the context! That reference is 1 Corinthians 14:34 "Let your women keep silence in the churches, for it is not permitted unto them to speak, but *they are commanded* to be under obedience as also saith the Law—and if they will learn any thing; let them ask their husbands at home—for it is a shame for women to speak in the church." Well, I guess that ends the discussion, doesn't it. No, it does not. First of all, the words 'they are commanded' are in italics meaning these words were added by the 1611 translators—all of which happened to have been men.

When Paul says this in his letter, he has already been talking for 32 previous verses about keeping GOOD ORDER in the church services which were being thronged by myriads of people. Remember, they did not have the audio-visual sound and light shows in huge auditoriums like we have today. These meetings were being held in a small building probably packed to standing room only, with the men near the front, then their women forming several rows behind the men. Farther back still were the Gentile 'seekers' that Paul wanted to reach with the Gospel. Apparently Paul is addressing the women who are asking their husbands about these new teachings—WHILE THE SERVICE IS GOING ON! As a professional teacher / instructor, I can tell you there is nothing so annoying and distracting to the rest of the class than having someone talking to another—even if they are whispering—while you are making your vital points. Paul is essentially trying to tell everyone to stay quiet so the Gentiles in the back can hear the Words of Life.

Further proof is found in the Book of Galatians where Paul discusses Sarah versus Hagar. The word choice by the master orator Paul is amazing. In the whole New Testament, the word for woman is 1135-gune-wife or woman; except for one time in Romans where childbearing is the topic—there it is 2538-kainotes-renewal.

In Galations, Paul is discussing Sarah versus Hagar—Sarah is described as the 'free-woman' in the King James Bible. The only issue is, if you look up woman in Strong's—at this verse: THERE IS NO WORD 'WOMAN' THERE! Paul says Sarah is simply the 'free'; while Hagar is described as the bond-woman (Strong's 3814)-paidiske-a female slave or servant.

Paul's main point is not the sex of the being in question (all men, male and female men, were under bondage to sin)—but the STATUS of the being—slave or free! Sarah was FREE—and bore Isaac who would father the FREE line of humankind. She willingly and voluntarily lined up behind Abraham and called him lord because he was following God, not because she was under a curse like Hagar was. A spiritual meaning is also intended here: Unsaved women that are still under the curse are not allowed to speak in a church meeting any more than an unsaved man still under the curse is allowed to. Two times in Scripture; devils—speaking through unsaved humans—are rebuked and exorcised. The one time it was a demon possessed male in the synagogue that Jesus cast out—and the other time it was a female slave that followed after Paul. ONLY those saved and called to preach the Good News may share the Gospel!

Paul says that in Christ there is no male or female! The implication is that IF a female human—bound under sin and subjected to a male for her own good—is freed by King Jesus. If such a woman lines up in support of Him—and, if married, with their husband's consent as co-regent: They are fully free to share the Good News like any other saved person! It is the devil himself that seeks to muzzle over half of the Christian Army!—yet many in Christendom go along with this deception!!

An example of how effective a free woman can potentially be is found in an account of Abraham Lincoln, the time when he bought a female slave. After the purchase, he instantly set her free! She said, 'So I can go anywhere I want?' Lincoln said, 'Yes.' She said, 'Then I think I will follow along with you.' She could do no better than to follow the one that set her free. Can you imagine the powerful witness this hopeless slave woman could provide to others similarly oppressed? Why would anyone except other slave owners want her to keep silence??

Ladies—once you are saved by King Jesus and He sets you free— you are restored to co-regency with any saved man. Yes, you are free to expound the Scriptures in church—even to pastor a church if God so calls you. If you want to be President of the United States or any other country—GO FOR IT! Margaret Thatcher did a magnificent job in leading England. Sarah Palin did a great job in Alaska as governor, just as Nikki Haley is doing a wonderful job as governor of South Carolina. Why would any open minded person think a woman could not be President of the United States? If she is saved; she, too—has the Third Person of Almighty God living in her as all Christians do—she has the same tools as any man that has accepted the Lord!

Men, if God so empowers a woman for any position a man traditionally occupies—MOVE OVER! The only possible exceptions I would offer would be hand-to-hand military confrontation. In this case, the need to win may depend on simple brute strength: Women SHOULD exercise wisdom and let the male of the species do it. After all, ladies—we men were made; YOU were 'specially crafted' for other purposes besides hand-to-hand conflict against a savage enemy.

On a lighter note: That old joke, 'What did God say when He made Adam?'—'I can do better than that!' is actually Biblically based!!

Another issue is the so-called 'Races' of humanity. Paul, when addressing the men of Athens in the Book of Acts says that all men were made of one blood. If this were true, then the science of DNA should show it to be true. What does this research reveal? ALL HUMANS share more than 99.9% the same DNA. We all have arms, hair, eyes, stomachs, toenails, etc. We all have skin—albeit of different levels of pigmentation. It is the DEVIL himself that takes 0.1% difference in DNA and causes all the racial hate and harm that has marred man's history. Remember, Jesus said if you hate your fellow man—you are a liar if you say you love God. You can hate their policies or politics or how they conduct their lives. You can oppose them in policy or politics or how they want you to conduct your life—but if you have the chance to witness Christ to them—you must!

Here is an example: There are many millions of 'illegal aliens' in the United States. We can and should have better control over our borders (policy and politics). We can and should identify who is here and send the bad ones home immediately or jail them (we have a right to protect ourselves and our society). However, those of them that are not already saved are bound under sin and headed for hell just as surely as any natural or naturalized citizen of the United States still under the curse is. While we grapple with these political issues—we can and MUST reach out to them for Jesus! You can get Spanish (or other language; there are sojourners from many nations here) New Testaments for a buck or two—and hand them out.

This world and all its woes are passing away. Their souls will suffer for eternity if we do not reach them before death. Could it be that God in His mercy and love for them BROUGHT THEM TO US—who have the Words of Life tucked away in our hearts—because we have been too lazy to GO TO THEM? Read the Old Testament!—you will find that God takes a pretty dim view of those who abuse 'those who have come to sojourn in the land'. The great grandmother of King David, ultimately the great, great, great . . . . grandmother of the Lord was an illegal alien come with Ruth to sojourn in Israel—hmmmm . . . .

Appendix VI

The Historical View of
The Book of Revelation
—particularly chapter 16

The Historical View of The Book of Revelation takes this entire narrative as a series of symbols—like when Daniel interpreted the symbol filled dreams of Nebuchadnezzar king of Babylon and Joseph the dreams of Pharaoh. The best explanation of those symbols—from Revelation chapter 1 up until chapter 16 are wonderfully explained in the book: <u>The Present Reign of Jesus Christ</u> by Robert Caringola. It is from chapter 16 on that I differ with his interpretation. He may be right and I may be wrong; more likely both of us are somewhat wrong—but since I am writing this book; I get to have my say. It is one of the wonderful things about living in a still free America!

Revelation chapter 16 begins the final judgments of God on unrepentant and rebellious men. There have been two great empires described as rising and falling in the Revelation thus far. These empires were the pagan Roman Empire that fell in 533 A.D. and the Papal Roman Empire that would last 1260 years (until 1793) when it would fall. The French Revolution destroyed the Papal Empire by destroying her first-born child that had been keeping her alive long beyond the time she should have fallen on her own. The first five vial judgments of Revelation 16:1-11 then break up the last lingering effects of this great empire by destroying her influence on the land, sea and political realms. It is the sixth vial that begins at verse twelve that ushers in the final incarnation of rebellious man's attempted usurpations of God's earth—of course, it is really satan behind all of these attempts.

Starting at Revelation 16:12—we see the symbolic 'Euphrates River' drying up—to make way for the kings of the east. This event sets for us the beginning date of the sixth vial somewhere between the years 1917 and 1923. It is the end of the Ottoman Empire as a result of World War I, the rise of the British Empire and the dividing of the land after war which is always done by the victors. The 'homeland' of the future nation of Israel was established by this declaration though it did not come into existence officially until 1948. The first attempt at uniting all nations of the earth followed this war with the League of Nations; the forerunner of the current United Nations.

The next verse has John seeing three unclean spirits like frogs; coming out of the mouth of the dragon (drakon), mouth of the beast (therion) and the mouth of the false prophet. The identity of the spirits as three frogs is significant for the French flag sported three toads— which later were converted to 'fleur-de-lis' symbols like the ones on the New Orleans Saints football team helmets. It appears the final attempt to usurp King Jesus' throne by satan using men will be a philosophy { . . . out of the mouth of . . . } and have aspects of these three characteristics: Out of the mouth of the Dragon—this philosophy will attract and mesmerize ungodly men, Out of the mouth of the Beast—this philosophy will be very dangerous and finally, Out of the mouth of the False Prophet—this philosophy will be a lie worthy of the devil himself. That philosophy is communism / socialism imposed by elitists—this philosophy was founded by none other than Karl Marx and given 'scientific cover' by Charles Darwin's infamous book On The Origin of Species.

It must also be pointed out that the symbols John sees—are ones not of his choosing, but of God's choosing. Frogs is not a commonly used word or important symbol in Hebrew history or prophecy. There are only 13 uses of 'frog(s)' in the Old Testament—every one of them in context refers to the Egyptian plague. There is only one use of frogs in the New Testament—here in Revelation 16. The point is: John likely is only a faithful recording reporter here; telling us exactly what he sees—it probably did not make sense to him either, but rather—would take on its special meaning as a marking point in history yet to play out. Daniel, too, was told simply to record what he was seeing—exactly as he saw it—though he did not understand it at the time. This helps us understand why men of every generation eagerly—perhaps too eagerly—misidentified the frogs symbol and heralded the Return of Jesus only to be disappointed. I am not too proud to think that the same could be true of my interpretation. It is very possible that my desire to be one of those still alive at His Coming has caused me to misidentify this symbol. I am only human after all.

However, this interpretation of mine DOES eerily fit the actual playing out of the events of today very, very well. So if I am right—and Jesus DOES show up soon—you heard it here first! Many are wondering if He will ever Return—which actually is a good thing! Why? Because it is prophesied that in the time men think not, THAT is when He will Come Again! Jesus said the days of His Return will be like the days of Noah just before the Flood.

Noah had been building that Ark for a while—and, we surmise, preaching to his neighbors about the judgment to come. They paid attention for a period of time, perhaps years—but tired of the wait. Perhaps the saddest situation was for those hired workers that actually helped build the Ark. When the job was done, those that had BEEN ON BOARD—walked off to the next job. If I am wrong and Jesus is another 200 years or more in arriving—oh, well! It is after all, only the Jewish year 5772—and if God is working off of a 7 'God-day' or 7000 year timeframe as many think—we must leave room for the 1000 year reign of Christ on earth—we are still about 228 years shy of 6000 years. I do take hope in the fact that Jesus said God the Father would shorten those 'man-days' near the end, for if He did not—no flesh would survive. My being wrong may bring some to Christ and for those that do not accept Him, will help fulfill prophecy by setting the stage further for those destined to not get on board Ark Jesus. The Ark is another Old Testament symbol of Christ's mission of salvation.

Ok—back to the theme of this chapter that was not intended to be in this book at all. The next verse tells us more—"for they are the spirits of devils (1142-daimon)". This word for devils is only used five times in the New Testament, three of the uses are in Revelation. What does it mean? It is defined as 'to distribute fortunes' with the implication that the fortunes distributed are not theirs to rightfully distribute. We are instructed in Revelation to look for a time when 'the re-distributors of wealth that is not theirs' occurs. Hmmm . . . . I remember a candidate for President of the United States say that he wanted to 'spread the wealth around . . . .' When this time comes, the installation of King

Jesus is at hand—and John is seeing symbols to allow faithful Christians to accurately identify the time that this would happen.

The result of the work of these devils is to take the 'kings of the earth and of the whole world' and 'to gather them to the battle of that great day of God Almighty.' The leaders of all bankrupt nations are gathering together to bail each other out (G-7 and G-10 nations; hmmm . . . the beast upon which the whore of Revelation 17 sits has seven heads and ten horns, must be just a coincidence . . .). America's Federal Reserve secretly and illegally transferred many hundreds of billions of dollars to Europe's socialist economies in 2010 / early 2011 to keep them afloat. The American Federal Reserve's unConstitutional 'Quantitative Easing 1 and 2' printed hundreds of billions more dollars that have no backing; ensuring massive inflation one day that will crush all average folks. Why not print more Federal Reserve Notes—they always were toilet paper—having NOTHING backing them up but the hot air of these 'kings of the earth'. The wise are fleeing to gold and silver and other items of intrinsic value—and storing food, water and other essentials.

In the next verse {Rev 16:15}, Jesus suddenly breaks into the narrative to warn of His imminent return "Behold!—I come as a thief . . ." In a short while, we shall see that the seventh and last vial judgment accomplishes the destruction of this cabal of rebellious kings of the earth with the result being the victory and installation of King Jesus as Lord of lords and King of kings.

The very next verse it the one everyone gets so wrapped up in—" . . . and He gathered them together into a place called in the Hebrew tongue: Armageddon." The 'He' in context must be understood to be God. It is God that is doing the gathering or allowing this gathering of kings in rebellion. Some say it is 'Anti-christ' doing the gathering—but this cannot be if one reads the entire narrative and maintains a consistent Historical View interpretation. Mr. Caringola's book identifies that the 'anti-Christ' was an entity from the prior empire that has fallen—and has no place in Chapter 16 events.

Since Revelation is ALL symbols—Armageddon must mean something! It does! The Scripture rightly points out that Armageddon is a Hebrew word—not a Greek word. When one consults Strong's—one finds it is actually two Hebrew words joined together—the only time in the entire Bible the word occurs. The two Hebrew words are 'har' and 'mageddon'. They mean: Har—mountains and Mageddon—rendezvous. Symbolically, Armageddon is to be a meeting of mountains—but what does this mean when the symbols are translated? In Hebrew prophecy, mountains are nations or kingdoms. Armageddon then would be a meeting of nations—the United Nations would fit.

What!? Yes, this organization is atheistic just as the French Revolution was. It's charter recognizes no God or gods—only the will of the collective. This organization is worldwide in influence—in other words: It is big enough to qualify—just like the two preceding Empires that rose and fell before it. It promotes communism / socialism more than anything else—a philosophy that is perfectly described by the characteristics set forth by John. Communism fascinates mankind generally. Communism is extremely dangerous. Communism is a lie worthy of the devil himself. Communism came out of the roots of the French Revolution. Communism appears at the right time in history—right after the drying up of the Euphrates River (end of the Ottoman Empire).

Until the election of 2008, the United States could—by itself—thwart the designs of this organization. With the results of that election—American resistance has been checked. We are now too bankrupt, too socially split, too weak militarily to stop the takeover. The condition of Armageddon is here—and no one recognizes it because everyone is looking for some kind of great battle near a small village in northern Israel. I have been to the site of ancient Meggiddo in the plain of Jezreel. It is a ruin under excavation—that is all. Yes, it was the most conquered and burned city in Israel during the many centuries it existed, but it is a place, not a symbol—and Armageddon is a symbol, not a place!

I know the sentence says, ' . . . gathered them into a place called . . . .'—but the word 'place' in Greek has a literal and a figurative meaning. The figurative meaning is 'condition'—so being consistent in interpretation, Armageddon would be a condition, not an actual place. The condition the kings of the earth are in is active rebellion against God's Son and rightful King of kings. Many have noted that the only religion that can be openly mocked without fear is true Biblical Christianity and faith in it's central figure Jesus Christ.

What comes next? Revelation 16:17 begins the seventh and last vial judgment. It is poured into the 'air'—the devil is said to be the prince of the power of the air. The Greek word for air can also be understood to be spirit—so the vial could be poured out on the spirit(s) that have usurped the throne of King Jesus.

The result of this pouring out is at first great clamor among the kings of the earth—and the greatest earthquake ever in the history of this planet. However, earthquakes are also symbols in Revelation; symbols of history altering political change. The first earthquake in Revelation destroys Pagan Rome with its aftershocks ushering in Papal Rome. The second earthquake destroys Papal Rome with its aftershocks ushering in the third Empire we now live in. This last earthquake HAS NO AFTERSHOCK!—for no more evil empires are ushered in! It is for this reason it is the biggest—it will END rebellious man's rule of this planet.

How will these wicked men be defeated? The vial also results in 'a great hail out of Heaven about the weight of a talent . . .' More symbols! What do they mean? The Greek word rendered in English as 'hail' means only 'a strike'—so this hail will be at least one (maybe more) 'strike(s)' so great that it (they) will be attributed to be an ACT OF GOD. They will ultimately break apart this world's ability to finance recovery. Has anything like this occurred? Hmmm . . . The tsunamis of 2000 and 2011; hurricane Katrina in America; the massive tornadoes this year in America, incredible flooding in one area with unquenchable fires in another, etc—the list is long and growing. Disasters so great, men attribute them to God.

However, I think these are just softening up blows before the main invasion. The reason I think this is because of WHAT hails down from heaven. Whatever it is—it is the 'weight of a talent . . . ' The word weight is the same word as talent in this verse. So the line should read in English, 'talent of a talent . . .'—but what could this mean? A talent was the largest denomination of money in the ancient world for many thousands of years. It was still in place when John received the Revelation. The strike talked of in this verse will break apart the worldwide economy so carefully pasted together behind the scenes by rebellious men for the last century or so. In my view, the owners of the Federal Reserves of America and the other major nations are these people this strike is directed against. This latest strike has caused the American Federal Reserve to have to buy back its worthless bonds on a massive 'propping up' scale. Last night (August 5, 2011)—Standard and Poor's credit rating agency made history by DOWNGRADING America's debt from AAA to AA+. This is the first time in American history that America has not had a AAA rating! This is yet another devastating blow to these 'puppet masters' behind the Federal Reserves of the world economy.

Revelation 16 ends and Revelation 17 picks up with an awestruck John needing an angel—one of the angels that had poured out a vial judgment no less—to come explain what he was seeing. That explanation takes the entirety of Revelation 17 and is filled with primarily ECONOMIC, not military, effects! The result is that these 'kings of the earth' turn on one another—and the beast they have created—and it self-destructs! This world economy is teetering on the verge of just such a worldwide economic disaster as I write this section that I was not going to include in this book. I believe Revelation 17 represents an interlude between the decision that effects the final strike and the occurrence of the actual strike. The American Congress and President have just signed the 'compromise' law that refused to deal with American debt issues and 'kicked the can' down the road until March of 2013 or a little after. Get ready folks!—we are in the interlude period provided by God's grace and mercy. There is nothing that will be done in time by fallible men to prevent the worldwide depression described in Revelation 17 & 18 (prediction in 17 & actual occurrence in 18).

Revelation 18 begins with Jesus proclaiming that Babylon the Great is fallen!—because it had become the habitation of devils (daimons— distributors of fortunes) and every foul bird . . . great; another symbol. The Greek word rendered 'bird' here means simply 'something that rises above the level plain'. A person who is an elitist—or thinks they are better, smarter, etc. than everyone else would fit nicely. The group that has put together this conglomeration of worldwide economic interdependence are often called elitists. Hmmmm . . . .

Revelation 18:4 is the long awaited RAPTURE—where God will either take His people out supernaturally or somehow shield them through this coming disaster. I am of the opinion that it will be a supernatural removal for the reasons I set forth in my other book: <u>Lumpy Oatmeal with Raisins and Cinnamon!</u> available from PublishAmerica. com. Folks, save yourself some money if you buy it. The softcover is $24.95 with the PAperback is $9.99—they are exactly the same thing. Yes, I just cut my profits on royalties by 60% so that you can have the TRUTH cheaper. The exact words are: "{18:4} And I heard another voice from Heaven saying, 'Come out of her, My people—that ye be not partakers of her sins and that ye receive not of her plagues.' In context, Jesus speaks the words of Revelation 18:1-3 and God the Father takes over at verse 18:4.

Later in Revelation 18:21—a mighty angel takes up a stone likened to a great millstone and casts it with violence into the sea. More symbols— the millstone was the center of economic activity in ancient times. Farmers grew grain and brought it to be milled, merchants bought the ground grain. The actual words in Greek mean the stone is hurled off a cliff. America's—and by extension the rest of the world's—economy is now routinely likened by commentators to a car hurtling towards a cliff—with everyone knowing it is going to happen, but no one doing much of anything to try to stop it.

If I were you, do two things. First, get saved so that YOU will either be taken with the rest of the saved or shielded from the worst of it— instead of having to share in the punishments to come. Second, saved or no—do what you can to get ready for whatever level of difficulty we are allowed to endure before the Return of Jesus Christ to be Everlasting King. Other sections of Revelation that I do not have time or space to deal with here indicate to me that we (the saved) may have to endure the opening phases of this calamity. God in His mercy may be having us store up supplies that can be used by those left behind who ransack our houses—so leave a Bible with your supplies; just in case God in His infinite mercy accepts repentance from those that waited too long.

God bless your reading this book and I hope to meet you all in Heaven!